HOW MARKETS
REALLY WORK

HOW MARKETS REALLY WORK

A Quantitative Guide to Stock Market Behavior

Laurence A. Connors

Conor Sen

Connors Research Group

TRADINGMARKETS™
PUBLISHING GROUP

ISBN 0-9755513-1-0

Printed in the United States of America.

Disclaimer

It should not be assumed that the methods, techniques, or indicators presented in this book will be profitable or that they will not result in losses. Past results are not necessarily indicative of future results. Examples in this book are for educational purposes only. The author, publishing firm, and any affiliates assume no responsibility for your trading results. This is not a solicitation of any order to buy or sell.

The NFA requires us to state that "HYPOTHETICAL OR SIMULATED PERFORMANCE RESULTS HAVE CERTAIN INHERENT LIMITATIONS. UNLIKE AN ACTUAL PERFORMANCE RECORD, SIMULATED RESULTS DO NOT REPRESENT ACTUAL TRADING. ALSO, SINCE THE TRADES HAVE NOT ACTUALLY BEEN EXECUTED, THE RESULTS MAY HAVE UNDER- OR OVERCOMPENSATED FOR THE IMPACT, IF ANY, OF CERTAIN MARKET FACTORS, SUCH AS LACK OF LIQUIDITY. SIMULATED TRADING PROGRAMS IN GENERAL ARE ALSO SUBJECT TO THE FACT THAT THEY ARE DESIGNED WITH THE BENEFIT OF HINDSIGHT. NO REPRESENTATION IS BEING MADE THAT ANY ACCOUNT WILL OR IS LIKELY TO ACHIEVE PROFITS OR LOSSES SIMILAR TO THOSE SHOWN."

To Bill James,
the inspiration behind this book.

CONTENTS

ACKNOWLEDGMENTS

■ ■

Special thanks to Ed Allen, Eddie Kwong, Brice Wightman, Judy Brown and Michael Chalapong for their assistance in helping us with this book.

CHAPTER 1

MARKET EDGES

■ ■

For many of us, Michael Lewis' 1989 best-selling book *Liar's Poker* was the first inside look at what day-to-day life was like at a major Wall Street trading firm. Lewis described in detail, the wheeling and dealing of some of the famous (and infamous) Wall Street titans who oversaw billions of dollars of transactions every trading day during the 1980s. The book remains a classic today but 14 years after it was published, Lewis outdid himself. In 2003, he published *Moneyball: The Art of Winning an Unfair Game.* The book chronicles the success of the Oakland A's, who under the guidance of their General Manager, Billy Beane, used massive amounts of statistical data to help them successfully run their ball team.

The A's essentially turned their backs on the old school of thinking, much of which was intuitive, and attempted to turn baseball into a science. Players who should have been 15th-round draft picks were being chosen by the A's near the top of the draft (and signed very cheaply). These types of players were chosen not because they "looked good" or the scouting reports said they "couldn't miss." They were chosen because the statistics said that these players had an edge and that this edge had a better chance of playing itself out than the "guessing" that had gone into past selections. Essentially, Billy Beane and the A's turned baseball upside down and by relying upon numbers instead of opinion, they have been able to successfully compete against teams that had far more money to spend on talent.

The godfather behind this move to relying upon numbers instead of gut is a brilliant gentleman by the name of Bill James. In the 1970s James began publishing studies and then books on player evaluation and baseball strategy. Up until a few years ago, James was all but ignored by mainstream baseball. Hall of Fame Manager Sparky Anderson, who is the only manager to win a World Series in both the National League and the American League, referred to James as "a fat guy with a beard who knows nothing about nothing." And in spite of the success that the A's and a few other teams have had relying upon statistics, the debate still rages as to its effectiveness. But, as this is being written, baseball has begun the process of turning away from the Sparky Anderson school of knowledge and accepting the thinking of people like Bill James. General Managers are being hired by teams not for their baseball playing careers nor their baseball prowess, but for their ability to analyze baseball statistics and make correct decisions using these statistics. Teams like the Red Sox and the Dodgers now have GMs who are only in their early thirties. Why are they entrusted with franchises that are valued in the hundreds of millions of dollars? It's because these guys don't guess. *They know numbers and their understanding of these numbers provides them with an edge.* And in some cases, this edge is substantial.

What does this have to do with trading? A lot. After we read *Moneyball*, we remarked that it's amazing that baseball has gone this route yet most of Wall Street still has not. If baseball has quantified mainstream parts of the game such as batting average, on base percentage, errors, steals, walks, etc., why hasn't Wall Street done the same with the indicators it relies upon every day? Trading day after trading day, we are bombarded with information from the media. "The market rose for the third straight day as the bulls are taking charge." What does this mean? It sounds good, doesn't it? It sure feels like the market is going to continue to rise. A market rising three days in a row is usually rising because of good news. Isn't that a precursor of things to come? What about advancing issues and declining issues? On days the market drops sharply and declining stocks far outnumber advancing stocks, the press and the analysts tell us this is bad. Poor market breadth is supposedly a sign of future weakness. It seems to make sense. But is it true? (You'll soon see it's not.)

Just as old school baseball used to think that a guy who was 6'3" and could run fast and hit the ball a mile was a "can't-miss prospect," much of old school Wall Street still thinks that good news and market strength is a sign of future upward price movement and bad news and poor market strength is a sign of future downward movement. As you will soon learn, at least looking at the market over the past 15 years (1989–2003), there is nothing further from the truth. This is not our opinion or guess. *It's what the statistics show.* And just as baseball had a tough time accepting the fact that on base percentage is more important than batting average, we suspect that many people on Wall Street, especially the media and the mainstream firms, will have a tough time accepting the fact that it's better over the near term for the market to have dropped than for it to have risen.

All combined, we have nearly three decades of trading and research experience behind us. Much of what you will learn from this book is a culmination of our work. We looked at a number of the most common ways traders, analysts and the press look at the market. Even though we went into the tests having a strong clue where the results would end up, even we were surprised at some of these results. The tests included us looking at how the S&P 500 cash market (SPX) and the Nasdaq 100 cash market (NDX) did over a 1-day, 2-day and 1-week period after they made a 5-period high, 10-period high, 5-period low and 10-period low (intraday). We also looked at how these markets did after prices rose multiple days in a row (showing strength) and declined multiple days in a row (showing weakness). We looked at the times when the markets made multiple-day higher highs and multiple-day lower lows, again looking at what happened after continuous strength and weakness. From there we looked at the days when the market rose sharply to the upside versus declined sharply to the downside.

Volume was another topic we tackled as it is one of the most often-used indicators. After volume, you'll learn about market breadth when we analyze what the market has done after advancing issues outperformed declining issues (and vice versa). The results from many of these chapters may surprise you and this chapter may be the biggest surprise.

From there, we looked at another common indicator: new 52-week highs and new 52-week lows. There's a healthy edge here and again, it's not where the analysts and the press say it is. In the final two chapters we'll show you how to use the put/call ratio and the VIX (CBOE Volatility Index). Each indicator has shown strong consistent edges and we'll teach you where these edges are.

Before we move to the next chapter and start looking at the test results, we'd like to cover a few guidelines to help you better understand how to use this book and how to use the information presented to help gain a greater edge in your trading and investing.

1. We'll state this again later in the book, but you need to know that there are no assurances that these test results will hold up in the future. Even though many of these tests are independent of one another and basically lead to the same conclusion, it cannot be assumed this conclusion (or any market conclusion) will hold true in the future.

2. Much of Wall Street is made up of opinions. It's also made up of opinions that are not backed by any statistical evidence. If the baseball world can do it then Wall Street can do it too. Hopefully this book is just the tip of the iceberg in using statistics to help understand how markets behave and how one can make proper and rational decisions on a day-to-day basis.

3. All these tests were run on the cash market and were not actual trades. Also, commissions and slippage were not factored in.

4. **All the tests use a benchmark.** This means we compared apples to apples. We looked at the results when certain situations occurred versus how the market performed on average during the same time period. We did the same for the percentage of trades that showed gains. In many cases we could have shown more test results but we didn't because the number of opportunities they occurred (the sample size) was too low.

5. We tested the S&P 500 and the Nasdaq 100 cash markets throughout the book.

6. Many of the tests run as far back as 15 years. This encompassed a solid bull market, followed by a very severe bear market, followed by a rally in 2003. The net bias was up for the entire time frame but the market also saw some healthy selling periods, especially from 2000–2002.

7. Finding clean market data is not as easy as one would think. There are data vendors whose data we could not trust. Therefore we used data from sources we trusted including the CBOE's for the put/call ratio tests and the VIX tests. In many cases we tested up to 15 years of data but in some cases we had to use fewer years in order not to compromise the integrity of the test results. These tests were run multiple times in order to assure the results. If you elect to do your own testing and find different results, it might possibly be due to the data your data vendor is providing.

8. In many chapters we also looked at the market trend. We defined the market trend as being up when the market was above its 200-day moving average (200-day ma) and down when it was below its 200-day moving average.

9. None of these tests are systems, nor should they be traded as systems, nor do we trade them alone as systems. They simply look at how markets behaved over a fixed period of time in specific market conditions.

10. This book can be used by everyone and should provide you with a basic philosophy for looking at the markets. Traders especially will be able to use this information as the focus of the book is on the short-term. But interestingly enough, you will see the same type of statistical evidence in long term investing using the basic philosophy and concepts from this book at www.AlwaysBuyValue.com (the site is related to us).

11. Please understand that the results you will see are average returns. This means that there were gains and losses in any individual trade that were far from average. And going forward, there will undoubtedly be situations that occur that will be far from the averages published here.

12. You'll see one common theme throughout this book: buying short-term weakness has outperformed buying short-term strength over the past 15 years. Should this trend continue, there is a big edge here for traders to take advantage of. The goal of this work is to show you when these times occurred and what the historical edge has been.

Let's now move ahead and look at specific market conditions.

CHAPTER 2

SHORT-TERM HIGHS AND SHORT-TERM LOWS

■ ■

Many traders and investors have been taught to buy strength and sell weakness. Buying new short-term highs is supposed to be the sign of a healthy market and selling new short-term lows is supposed to be the sign of a weak market. Our results over a 15-year period show the exact opposite.

The highlights of the results include the fact that buying new 10-day highs in the S&P 500 lost money when exiting one week later. In a powerful bull market, you would have actually lost money by buying these new highs and exiting a week later. Said another way, prices on average have been lower, not higher, one week after the market has made a short-term new high.

Let's now look at a few of our test results.

The Market Has Declined (on Average) Following 5- and 10-Day Highs

1. First we looked at the S&P 500 from January 1, 1989 through December 31, 2003. We then looked at how the SPX performed every day during that period of time. We found that the SPX had gained an aver-

age of .04% per day and an average of .19% per week for the 15-year period, reflecting the bull market move.

We then looked at the average daily gain of the SPX after it made a new 5-day (intraday) high. Remember, new highs are supposedly a sign of strength, are "breakouts," and are considered by many a time to buy. What we found was the opposite. These new highs underperformed the average daily market. Their average daily gain for the next day was half, coming in at .02%. We also looked at how these "breakouts" did over the next week and again we see them performing poorly. **In fact, the average 1-week gain was .03%, far less than the average weekly gain of .19% over the same time period.**

Ten-day new highs, which are considered even stronger markets to be buying, showed even worse results. Their average daily gain after the SPX made a new 10-day high was .00%. The weekly results were just as poor, also showing no gain.

Returns Increased Following 5- and 10-Day Losses

2. We then looked at when markets were acting poorly. We looked at the performance of the SPX after it made a new 5-day low. Again, our findings were completely at odds with conventional teachings. We found that the average daily gain after a 5-day low was .06%. The average weekly gain was .47%, outperforming the average week and far outperforming the week following a new 5-day high. The 10-day new lows showed similar performance. The average daily gain following a 10-day new low was .12% and .56% for the weekly gain.

New Highs Made Under the 200-Day Moving Average Strongly Underperformed

3. We also looked at the impact that trend had with a market making a new short-term high versus a new short-term low. We found that, buying a new 5-day high when the SPX was trading under its 200-day moving average showed a 1-day return of –.04% and only a small 1-week gain of .01%. Ten-day new highs lost money both the next day (–.05%) and the next week (–.12%). These results show that "bear traps" do exist when markets rally while trading under their 200-day moving average and you would probably be wise to avoid buying equities during these days.

Pullbacks Within the Direction of the Trend Are Significant. Rallies Counter to the Trend Underperformed

4. When you combine both price movement with trend, you see additional significant results. For example, when a 10-day low occurred in the S&P 500, when it was above its 200-day moving average, it led to higher prices 60.49% of the time the next day. When the index made a 10-day high below the 200-day moving average, prices rose only 46.8% of the time the next day.

Now let's look at the bar graphs, time charts, and the entire test results of how the SPX and the NDX have performed after making 5-day highs, 10-day highs, 5-day lows, and 10-day lows.

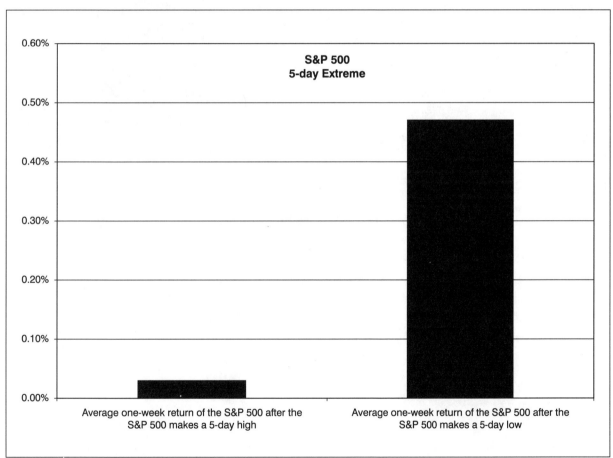

Figure 2-1　　1989–2003

5-Day Lows in the S&P 500 Significantly Outperformed 5-Day Highs

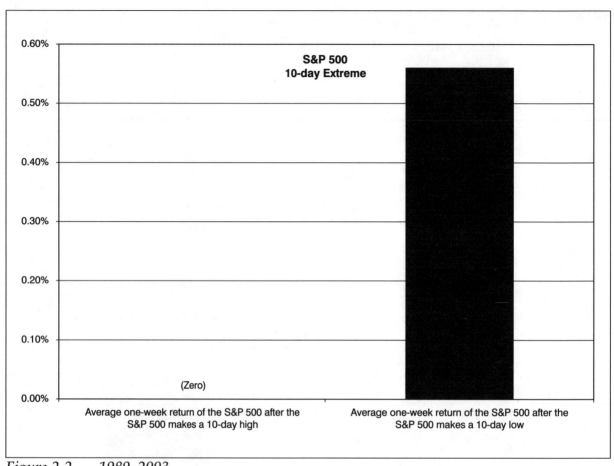

Figure 2-2   1989–2003

10-Day Lows in the S&P 500 Greatly Outperformed 10-Day Highs

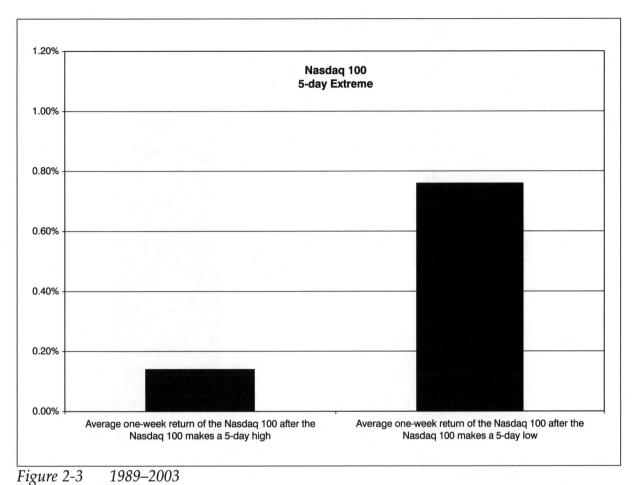

Figure 2-3   1989–2003

New 5-Day Highs in the Nasdaq Underperformed versus 5-Day Lows

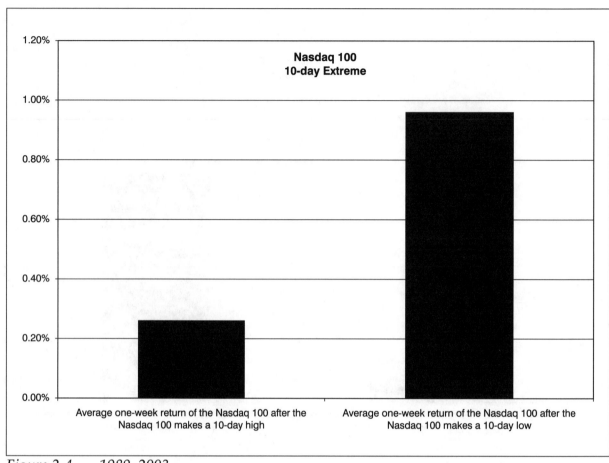

Figure 2-4   1989–2003

Nasdaq 100 10-Day Lows Outperformed 10-Day Highs by a Better Than 3-1 Margin

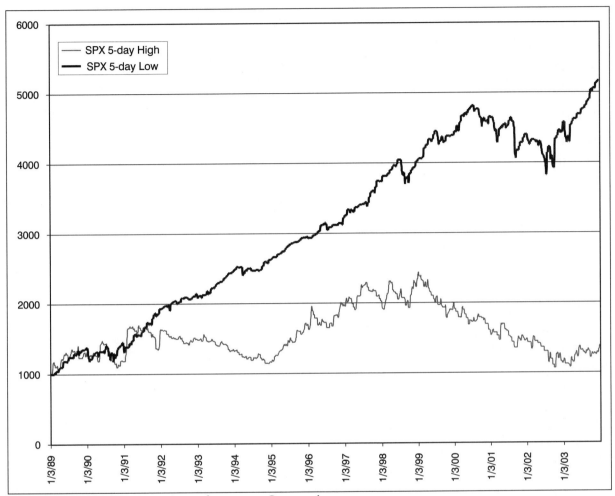

Figure 2-5   Time Graph Performance Comparison

All time graphs in this book use a one-week exit.

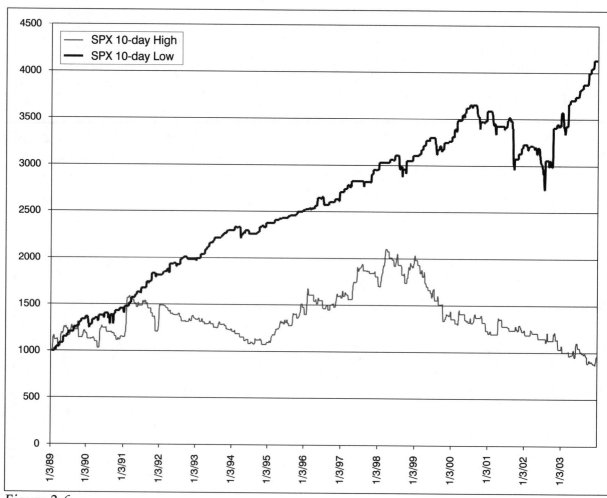

Figure 2-6

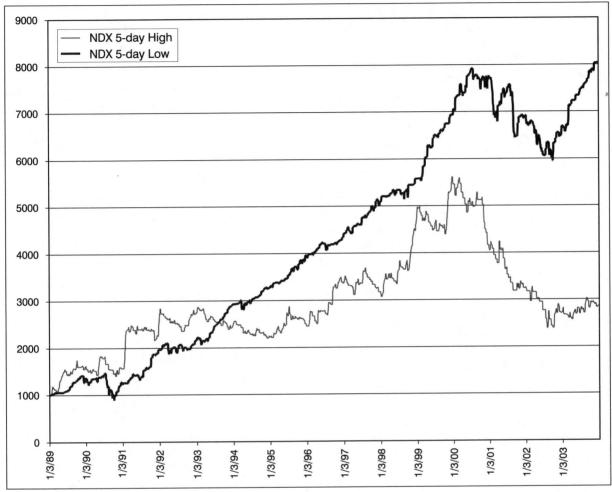

Figure 2-7

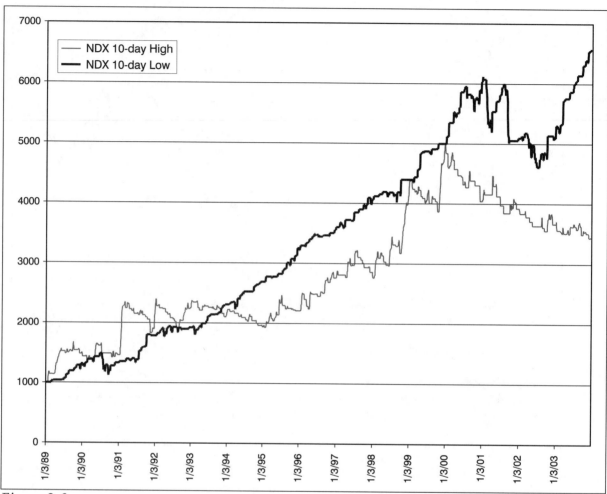

Figure 2-8

TABLE EXPLANATION

(see tables next page)

Following is an explanation of each of the columns in the tables that appear at the end of each chapter.

1. The "Index" column indicates which market we tested, either the S&P 500 (SPX) or the Nasdaq 100 (NDX).

2. "Rule 1" describes the first rule of the test. We would take a position only if this condition occurred.

3. "Rule 2" is the second rule of the test, if applicable. If this column contains information, then both rule 1 and rule 2 must be in place to take a position. If this column is blank, then only rule 1 is needed.

4. The "Time Period" column indicates the length of a single test. "1 day" means buy today, sell tomorrow. "1 week" means buy today, exit five trading days from now.

5. The "Gain/Loss" column lists the average percentage gain or loss the market made while we were in the position with the specified rules.

6. In every test we wanted to have a baseline for comparison. We called this our "Benchmark Average." The benchmark average is the average percentage the market gained or lost during the specified time period over all length of the test interval. For instance, the average one-day gain of the S&P 500 from 1989 to 2003 was 0.04%.

7. The "# Winners" column tallies up the number of profitable tests for the given set of rules.

8. The "# Days" column tallies up the number of times that our set of rules produced a trade.

9. The "% Profitable" column is simply the number of winners divided by the total number of trades.

10. The "% Profitable Benchmark" column serves as a profitability comparison between our trade signal and the typical market. It takes all market periods and calculates what percentage of them were profitable.

	1	2	3	4	5	6	7	8	9	10
	Index	Rule 1	Rule 2	Time Period	Gain/Loss	Benchmark Avg	# Winners	# Days	% Profitable	% Profitable Benchmark
	SPX	5-day high		1 day	0.02%	0.04%	655	1296	50.54%	52.71%
	SPX	5-day high		2 days	0.01%	0.08%	675	1295	52.12%	54.11%
	SPX	5-day high		1 week	0.03%	0.21%	699	1294	54.02%	56.66%
	SPX	10-day high		1 day	0.00%	0.04%	465	950	48.95%	52.71%
	SPX	10-day high		2 days	-0.03%	0.08%	479	949	50.47%	54.11%
	SPX	10-day high		1 week	0.00%	0.21%	506	947	53.43%	56.66%
	SPX	1-month high		1 day	0.02%	0.04%	359	719	49.93%	52.71%
	SPX	1-month high		2 days	0.02%	0.08%	370	718	51.53%	54.11%
	SPX	1-month high		1 week	0.01%	0.21%	384	716	53.63%	56.66%
	SPX	5-day low		1 day	0.06%	0.04%	483	886	54.51%	52.71%
	SPX	5-day low		2 days	0.16%	0.08%	490	886	55.30%	54.11%
	SPX	5-day low		1 week	0.47%	0.21%	533	887	60.09%	56.66%
	SPX	10-day low		1 day	0.12%	0.04%	317	557	56.91%	52.71%
	SPX	10-day low		2 days	0.25%	0.08%	320	557	57.45%	54.11%
	SPX	10-day low		1 week	0.56%	0.21%	333	557	59.78%	56.66%
	SPX	1-month low		1 day	0.15%	0.04%	188	331	56.80%	52.71%
	SPX	1-month low		2 days	0.31%	0.08%	198	331	59.82%	54.11%
	SPX	1-month low		1 week	0.59%	0.21%	191	331	57.70%	56.66%
	SPX	5-day high	Above 200-day MA	1 day	0.03%	0.05%	492	969	50.77%	53.49%
	SPX	5-day high	Above 200-day MA	2 days	0.02%	0.10%	511	968	52.79%	55.56%
	SPX	5-day high	Above 200-day MA	1 week	0.01%	0.25%	514	967	53.15%	58.22%
	SPX	10-day high	Above 200-day MA	1 day	0.00%	0.05%	359	735	48.84%	53.49%
	SPX	10-day high	Above 200-day MA	2 days	-0.03%	0.10%	375	734	51.09%	55.56%
	SPX	10-day high	Above 200-day MA	1 week	0.00%	0.25%	384	732	52.46%	58.22%
	SPX	1-month high	Above 200-day MA	1 day	0.02%	0.05%	290	582	49.83%	53.49%
	SPX	1-month high	Above 200-day MA	2 days	0.02%	0.10%	306	581	52.67%	55.56%
	SPX	1-month high	Above 200-day MA	1 week	0.07%	0.25%	310	579	53.54%	58.22%
	SPX	5-day low	Above 200-day MA	1 day	0.07%	0.05%	290	516	56.20%	53.49%
	SPX	5-day low	Above 200-day MA	2 days	0.20%	0.10%	297	516	57.56%	55.56%
	SPX	5-day low	Above 200-day MA	1 week	0.59%	0.25%	338	517	65.38%	58.22%
	SPX	10-day low	Above 200-day MA	1 day	0.14%	0.05%	173	286	60.49%	53.49%
	SPX	10-day low	Above 200-day MA	2 days	0.31%	0.10%	171	286	59.79%	55.56%
	SPX	10-day low	Above 200-day MA	1 week	0.66%	0.25%	190	286	66.43%	58.22%
	SPX	1-month low	Above 200-day MA	1 day	0.13%	0.05%	83	136	61.03%	53.49%
	SPX	1-month low	Above 200-day MA	2 days	0.33%	0.10%	85	136	62.50%	55.56%
	SPX	1-month low	Above 200-day MA	1 week	0.63%	0.25%	89	136	65.44%	58.22%
	SPX	5-day high	Below 200-day MA	1 day	-0.04%	0.02%	113	241	46.89%	50.63%
	SPX	5-day high	Below 200-day MA	2 days	-0.05%	0.04%	114	241	47.30%	50.24%
	SPX	5-day high	Below 200-day MA	1 week	0.01%	0.09%	125	241	51.87%	52.48%
	SPX	10-day high	Below 200-day MA	1 day	-0.05%	0.02%	66	141	46.81%	50.63%
	SPX	10-day high	Below 200-day MA	2 days	-0.10%	0.04%	63	141	44.68%	50.24%
	SPX	10-day high	Below 200-day MA	1 week	-0.12%	0.09%	73	141	51.77%	52.48%
	SPX	1-month high	Below 200-day MA	1 day	0.06%	0.02%	42	83	50.60%	50.63%
	SPX	1-month high	Below 200-day MA	2 days	0.03%	0.04%	38	83	45.78%	50.24%
	SPX	1-month high	Below 200-day MA	1 week	-0.29%	0.09%	42	83	50.60%	52.48%
	SPX	5-day low	Below 200-day MA	1 day	0.06%	0.02%	174	337	51.63%	50.63%
	SPX	5-day low	Below 200-day MA	2 days	0.11%	0.04%	176	337	52.23%	50.24%
	SPX	5-day low	Below 200-day MA	1 week	0.24%	0.09%	172	337	51.04%	52.48%
	SPX	10-day low	Below 200-day MA	1 day	0.10%	0.02%	127	248	51.21%	50.63%
	SPX	10-day low	Below 200-day MA	2 days	0.17%	0.04%	135	248	54.44%	50.24%
	SPX	10-day low	Below 200-day MA	1 week	0.37%	0.09%	125	248	50.40%	52.48%
	SPX	1-month low	Below 200-day MA	1 day	0.15%	0.02%	101	191	52.88%	50.63%
	SPX	1-month low	Below 200-day MA	2 days	0.29%	0.04%	110	191	57.59%	50.24%
	SPX	1-month low	Below 200-day MA	1 week	0.51%	0.09%	98	191	51.31%	52.48%

1	2	3	4	5	6	7	8	9	10
Index	Rule 1	Rule 2	Time Period	Gain/Loss	Benchmark Avg	# Winners	# Days	% Profitable	% Profitable Benchmark
NDX	5-day high		1 day	0.08%	0.08%	712	1292	55.11%	54.14%
NDX	5-day high		2 days	0.11%	0.15%	690	1292	53.41%	53.43%
NDX	5-day high		1 week	0.14%	0.37%	711	1291	55.07%	56.36%
NDX	10-day high		1 day	0.08%	0.08%	531	950	55.89%	54.14%
NDX	10-day high		2 days	0.12%	0.15%	508	950	53.47%	53.43%
NDX	10-day high		1 week	0.26%	0.37%	520	949	54.79%	56.36%
NDX	1-month high		1 day	0.06%	0.08%	392	699	56.08%	54.14%
NDX	1-month high		2 days	0.15%	0.15%	382	699	54.65%	53.43%
NDX	1-month high		1 week	0.20%	0.37%	384	699	54.94%	56.36%
NDX	5-day low		1 day	0.15%	0.08%	508	924	54.98%	54.14%
NDX	5-day low		2 days	0.28%	0.15%	513	927	55.34%	53.43%
NDX	5-day low		1 week	0.76%	0.37%	546	927	58.90%	56.36%
NDX	10-day low		1 day	0.33%	0.08%	318	576	55.21%	54.14%
NDX	10-day low		2 days	0.45%	0.15%	327	578	56.57%	53.43%
NDX	10-day low		1 week	0.96%	0.37%	354	578	61.25%	56.36%
NDX	1-month low		1 day	0.38%	0.08%	181	329	55.02%	54.14%
NDX	1-month low		2 days	0.54%	0.15%	187	331	56.50%	53.43%
NDX	1-month low		1 week	0.89%	0.37%	204	331	61.63%	56.36%
NDX	5-day high	Above 200-day MA	1 day	0.12%	0.09%	531	958	55.43%	54.96%
NDX	5-day high	Above 200-day MA	2 days	0.20%	0.19%	520	958	54.28%	54.80%
NDX	5-day high	Above 200-day MA	1 week	0.30%	0.49%	530	957	55.38%	58.40%
NDX	10-day high	Above 200-day MA	1 day	0.11%	0.09%	419	745	56.24%	54.96%
NDX	10-day high	Above 200-day MA	2 days	0.15%	0.19%	401	745	53.83%	54.80%
NDX	10-day high	Above 200-day MA	1 week	0.30%	0.49%	408	744	54.84%	58.40%
NDX	1-month high	Above 200-day MA	1 day	0.10%	0.09%	320	565	56.64%	54.96%
NDX	1-month high	Above 200-day MA	2 days	0.20%	0.19%	308	565	54.51%	54.80%
NDX	1-month high	Above 200-day MA	1 week	0.27%	0.49%	309	565	54.69%	58.40%
NDX	5-day low	Above 200-day MA	1 day	0.11%	0.09%	285	511	55.77%	54.96%
NDX	5-day low	Above 200-day MA	2 days	0.35%	0.19%	298	511	58.32%	54.80%
NDX	5-day low	Above 200-day MA	1 week	1.02%	0.49%	319	511	62.43%	58.40%
NDX	10-day low	Above 200-day MA	1 day	0.30%	0.09%	159	273	58.24%	54.96%
NDX	10-day low	Above 200-day MA	2 days	0.60%	0.19%	169	273	61.90%	54.80%
NDX	10-day low	Above 200-day MA	1 week	1.30%	0.49%	184	273	67.40%	58.40%
NDX	1-month low	Above 200-day MA	1 day	0.29%	0.09%	66	108	61.11%	54.96%
NDX	1-month low	Above 200-day MA	2 days	0.66%	0.19%	70	108	64.81%	54.80%
NDX	1-month low	Above 200-day MA	1 week	0.96%	0.49%	71	108	65.74%	58.40%
NDX	5-day high	Below 200-day MA	1 day	-0.10%	0.03%	126	242	52.07%	52.03%
NDX	5-day high	Below 200-day MA	2 days	-0.32%	0.04%	115	242	47.52%	49.91%
NDX	5-day high	Below 200-day MA	1 week	-0.68%	0.06%	115	242	47.52%	51.13%
NDX	10-day high	Below 200-day MA	1 day	-0.11%	0.03%	70	134	52.24%	52.03%
NDX	10-day high	Below 200-day MA	2 days	-0.18%	0.04%	64	134	47.76%	49.91%
NDX	10-day high	Below 200-day MA	1 week	-0.25%	0.06%	61	134	45.52%	51.13%
NDX	1-month high	Below 200-day MA	1 day	-0.30%	0.03%	36	76	47.37%	52.03%
NDX	1-month high	Below 200-day MA	2 days	-0.32%	0.04%	38	76	50.00%	49.91%
NDX	1-month high	Below 200-day MA	1 week	-0.69%	0.06%	32	76	42.11%	51.13%
NDX	5-day low	Below 200-day MA	1 day	0.21%	0.03%	202	378	53.44%	52.03%
NDX	5-day low	Below 200-day MA	2 days	0.19%	0.04%	194	381	50.92%	49.91%
NDX	5-day low	Below 200-day MA	1 week	0.38%	0.06%	201	381	52.76%	51.13%
NDX	10-day low	Below 200-day MA	1 day	0.37%	0.03%	151	285	52.98%	52.03%
NDX	10-day low	Below 200-day MA	2 days	0.31%	0.04%	148	287	51.57%	49.91%
NDX	10-day low	Below 200-day MA	1 week	0.62%	0.06%	156	287	54.36%	51.13%
NDX	1-month low	Below 200-day MA	1 day	0.45%	0.03%	113	215	52.56%	52.03%
NDX	1-month low	Below 200-day MA	2 days	0.49%	0.04%	113	217	52.07%	49.91%
NDX	1-month low	Below 200-day MA	1 week	0.86%	0.06%	129	217	59.45%	51.13%

SUMMARY AND CONCLUSION

As you can see, the greater opportunity and edge lies in being a buyer as the market makes a new short-term low versus buying when it makes a new high. Why is this so? It's likely because a market usually makes a new high "after" good news has occurred. This good news could be economic reports, earnings and more. The buying has "already occurred." On the opposite side, new lows are usually accompanied by bad economic news, bad earnings, etc. The sellers have taken prices lower and from there, the buyers get to step in, especially those correctly anticipating better news in the near future.

In conclusion, the statistics show that it has been better to be a buyer of new short-term lows, rather than a buyer of new short-term highs (breakouts).

Now let's look at the times when the market has made multiple days of higher highs and multiple days of lower lows.

CHAPTER 3

HIGHER HIGHS AND LOWER LOWS

■ ■

The questions we asked here were, "Is it better to be a buyer after the market has been strong and has made multiple days of higher highs? And, is it better to be a seller after the market has shown signs of weakness and has made multiple days of lower lows?"

It is generally accepted that markets that make multiple higher highs in a row are strong and markets that make multiple lower lows in a row are weak. A higher high simply means that today's intraday high (not close) was higher than yesterday's intraday high. A lower low means that today's intraday low was lower than yesterday's intraday low.

In this chapter, we look at the times when the SPX and the NDX (separately) made 3 or more days of higher highs. During these times the market is behaving strongly. Yesterday's high was above the previous day's high and today's high is even higher. We also look at the times when the SPX and the NDX made 3 or more lower lows. These are usually selling days and these selling days are supposedly a sign of future weakness.

We looked at the market over a 15-year period (1989–2003) and a summary of our findings is as follows:

The Market Lost Money Within One Week After 3 or More Consecutive Days of Higher Highs

1. After the market made 3 or more higher highs, it underperformed the average daily market return over the next 2 trading days and especially the next week. **In fact, the S&P 500 has lost money (net) within a week after making a 3- or more-day higher high (again, in spite of an upward market bias).**

Multiple Days of Lower Lows Outperformed the Average Daily Gain

2. The opposite is true for lows. Weakness, as defined by the market making multiple day lows, is followed on average by strength. Three, 4, and 5 days in a row lows outperform the average day after 1 day, 2 days, and 1 week.

Multiple-Day Lows Far Outperformed Multiple-Day Highs

3. This is most significant: When we matched up what the market did after making multiple higher highs versus making multiple lower lows, we see significant edges. For example, when the market makes 5 lower lows in a row, the average weekly gain has been .79% (better than triple the average weekly gain for all time periods). When it has made 5 higher highs in a row, the market on average has lost .21% over the next week.

Multiple-Day Lows in the Nasdaq Outperformed Multiple-Day Highs

4. The same types of results are seen when looking at the Nasdaq 100. Multiple-day lows outperform multiple-day highs by a wide per trade margin.

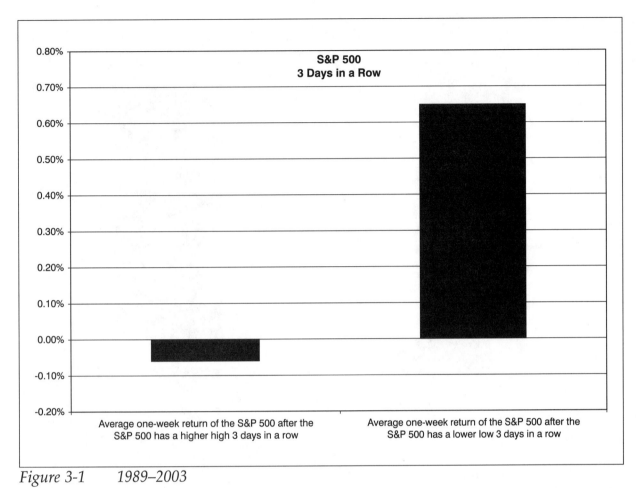

Figure 3-1   1989–2003

3 Consecutive Days Higher Highs in the S&P 500 Has Led on Average to Negative Returns After 1 Week

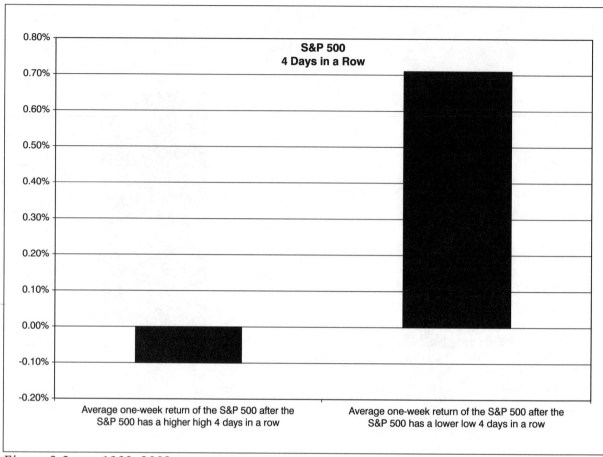

Figure 3-2   1989–2003

4 Consecutive Days of Lower Lows Has Led to Returns Far Greater Than
4 Consecutive Days of Higher Highs

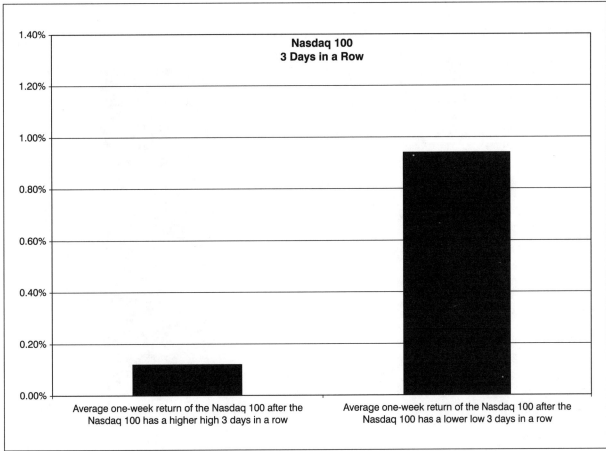

Figure 3-3   *1989–2003*

3 Consecutive Days of Lower Lows in the Nasdaq Has Led (on Average) to Returns Approximately 6 Times Greater Than 3 Consecutive Higher Highs After 1 Week

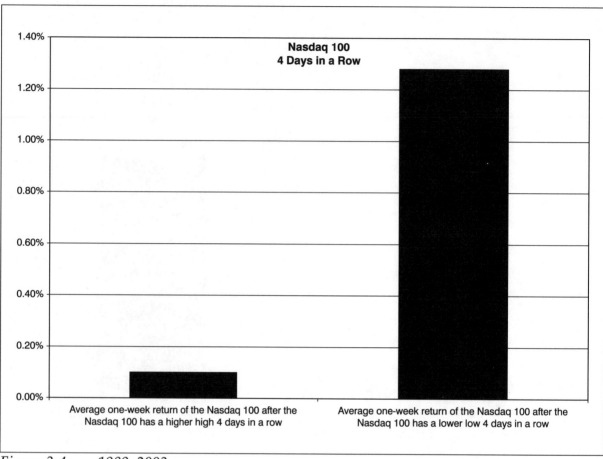

Figure 3-4   1989–2003

4 Consecutive Days of Lower Lows in the Nasdaq Has Led (on Average) to Returns of Approximately 12-1 Better Than 4 Consecutive Days of Higher Highs After 1 Week

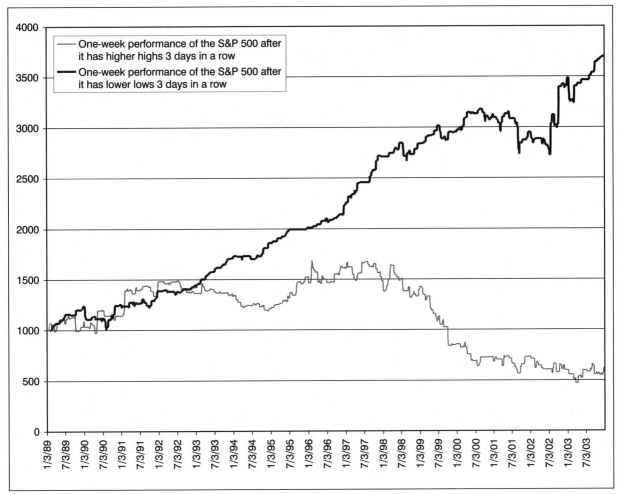

Figure 3-5

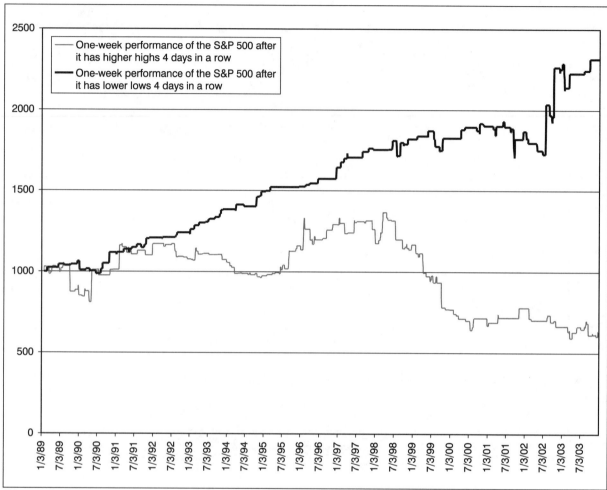

Figure 3-6

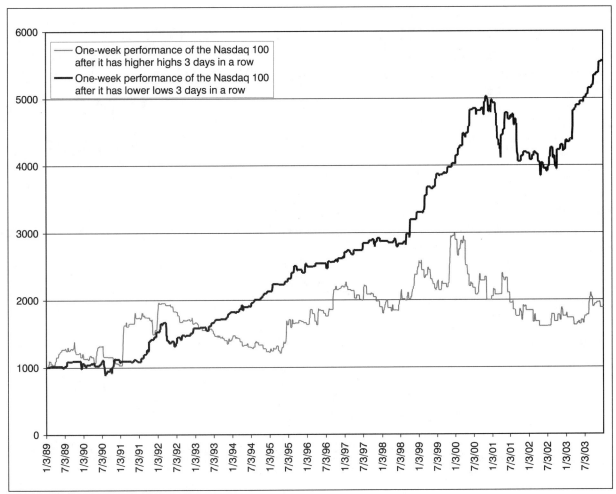

Figure 3-7

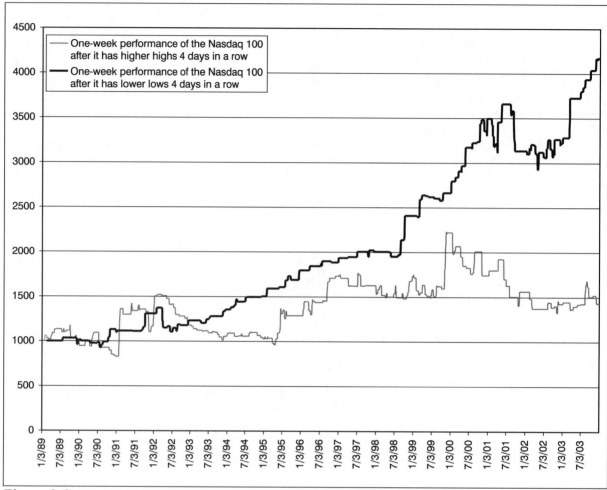

Figure 3-8

Index	Rule 1	Rule 2	Time Period	Gain/Loss	Benchmark Avg	# Winners	# Days	% Profitable	% Profitable Benchmark
SPX	Higher high 3 days in a row		1 day	0.02%	0.04%	329	649	50.69%	52.71%
SPX	Higher high 3 days in a row		2 days	0.03%	0.08%	348	649	53.62%	54.11%
SPX	Higher high 3 days in a row		1 week	-0.06%	0.21%	350	649	53.93%	56.66%
SPX	Higher high 4 days in a row		1 day	0.05%	0.04%	193	364	53.02%	52.71%
SPX	Higher high 4 days in a row		2 days	0.03%	0.08%	195	364	53.57%	54.11%
SPX	Higher high 4 days in a row		1 week	-0.10%	0.21%	191	364	52.47%	56.66%
SPX	Higher high 5 days in a row		1 day	0.03%	0.04%	102	210	48.57%	52.71%
SPX	Higher high 5 days in a row		2 days	0.04%	0.08%	105	210	50.00%	54.11%
SPX	Higher high 5 days in a row		1 week	-0.15%	0.21%	110	210	52.38%	56.66%
SPX	Lower low 3 days in a row		1 day	0.17%	0.04%	244	414	58.94%	52.71%
SPX	Lower low 3 days in a row		2 days	0.29%	0.08%	242	415	58.31%	54.11%
SPX	Lower low 3 days in a row		1 week	0.65%	0.21%	259	415	62.41%	56.66%
SPX	Lower low 4 days in a row		1 day	0.18%	0.04%	105	185	56.76%	52.71%
SPX	Lower low 4 days in a row		2 days	0.41%	0.08%	115	185	62.16%	54.11%
SPX	Lower low 4 days in a row		1 week	0.71%	0.21%	116	185	62.70%	56.66%
SPX	Lower low 5 days in a row		1 day	0.43%	0.04%	56	86	65.12%	52.71%
SPX	Lower low 5 days in a row		2 days	0.58%	0.08%	59	86	68.60%	54.11%
SPX	Lower low 5 days in a row		1 week	0.79%	0.21%	51	86	59.30%	56.66%
SPX	Higher high 3 days in a row	Above 200-day MA	1 day	0.04%	0.05%	281	545	51.56%	53.49%
SPX	Higher high 3 days in a row	Above 200-day MA	2 days	0.04%	0.10%	299	545	54.86%	55.56%
SPX	Higher high 3 days in a row	Above 200-day MA	1 week	-0.08%	0.25%	292	545	53.58%	58.22%
SPX	Higher high 4 days in a row	Above 200-day MA	1 day	0.06%	0.05%	171	318	53.77%	53.49%
SPX	Higher high 4 days in a row	Above 200-day MA	2 days	0.01%	0.10%	171	318	53.77%	55.56%
SPX	Higher high 4 days in a row	Above 200-day MA	1 week	-0.14%	0.25%	165	318	51.89%	58.22%
SPX	Higher high 5 days in a row	Above 200-day MA	1 day	0.03%	0.05%	92	189	48.68%	53.49%
SPX	Higher high 5 days in a row	Above 200-day MA	2 days	0.02%	0.10%	94	189	49.74%	55.56%
SPX	Higher high 5 days in a row	Above 200-day MA	1 week	-0.17%	0.25%	100	189	52.91%	58.22%
SPX	Lower low 3 days in a row	Above 200-day MA	1 day	0.24%	0.05%	152	240	63.33%	53.49%
SPX	Lower low 3 days in a row	Above 200-day MA	2 days	0.43%	0.10%	151	241	62.66%	55.56%
SPX	Lower low 3 days in a row	Above 200-day MA	1 week	0.77%	0.25%	171	241	70.95%	58.22%
SPX	Lower low 4 days in a row	Above 200-day MA	1 day	0.21%	0.05%	59	96	61.46%	53.49%
SPX	Lower low 4 days in a row	Above 200-day MA	2 days	0.40%	0.10%	62	96	64.58%	55.56%
SPX	Lower low 4 days in a row	Above 200-day MA	1 week	0.60%	0.25%	70	96	72.92%	58.22%
SPX	Lower low 5 days in a row	Above 200-day MA	1 day	0.40%	0.05%	26	37	70.27%	53.49%
SPX	Lower low 5 days in a row	Above 200-day MA	2 days	0.46%	0.10%	27	37	72.97%	55.56%
SPX	Lower low 5 days in a row	Above 200-day MA	1 week	0.40%	0.25%	25	37	67.57%	58.22%
SPX	Higher high 3 days in a row	Below 200-day MA	1 day	-0.06%	0.02%	48	104	46.15%	50.63%
SPX	Higher high 3 days in a row	Below 200-day MA	2 days	-0.04%	0.04%	49	104	47.12%	50.24%
SPX	Higher high 3 days in a row	Below 200-day MA	1 week	0.06%	0.09%	58	104	55.77%	52.48%
SPX	Higher high 4 days in a row	Below 200-day MA	1 day	0.00%	0.02%	22	46	47.83%	50.63%
SPX	Higher high 4 days in a row	Below 200-day MA	2 days	0.13%	0.04%	24	46	52.17%	50.24%
SPX	Higher high 4 days in a row	Below 200-day MA	1 week	0.16%	0.09%	26	46	56.52%	52.48%
SPX	Higher high 5 days in a row	Below 200-day MA	1 day	0.05%	0.02%	10	21	47.62%	50.63%
SPX	Higher high 5 days in a row	Below 200-day MA	2 days	0.25%	0.04%	11	21	52.38%	50.24%
SPX	Higher high 5 days in a row	Below 200-day MA	1 week	0.11%	0.09%	10	21	47.62%	52.48%
SPX	Lower low 3 days in a row	Below 200-day MA	1 day	0.07%	0.02%	92	174	52.87%	50.63%
SPX	Lower low 3 days in a row	Below 200-day MA	2 days	0.09%	0.04%	91	174	52.30%	50.24%
SPX	Lower low 3 days in a row	Below 200-day MA	1 week	0.48%	0.09%	88	174	50.57%	52.48%
SPX	Lower low 4 days in a row	Below 200-day MA	1 day	0.16%	0.02%	46	89	51.69%	50.63%
SPX	Lower low 4 days in a row	Below 200-day MA	2 days	0.41%	0.04%	53	89	59.55%	50.24%
SPX	Lower low 4 days in a row	Below 200-day MA	1 week	0.83%	0.09%	46	89	51.69%	52.48%
SPX	Lower low 5 days in a row	Below 200-day MA	1 day	0.46%	0.02%	30	49	61.22%	50.63%
SPX	Lower low 5 days in a row	Below 200-day MA	2 days	0.67%	0.04%	32	49	65.31%	50.24%
SPX	Lower low 5 days in a row	Below 200-day MA	1 week	1.08%	0.09%	26	49	53.06%	52.48%

See page 17 for column descriptions.

Index	Rule 1	Rule 2	Time Period	Gain/Loss	Benchmark Avg	# Winners	# Days	% Profitable	% Profitable Benchmark
NDX	Higher high 3 days in a row		1 day	0.06%	0.08%	392	724	54.14%	54.14%
NDX	Higher high 3 days in a row		2 days	0.08%	0.15%	381	722	52.77%	53.46%
NDX	Higher high 3 days in a row		1 week	0.12%	0.37%	396	723	54.77%	56.36%
NDX	Higher high 4 days in a row		1 day	0.00%	0.08%	228	429	53.15%	54.14%
NDX	Higher high 4 days in a row		2 days	-0.02%	0.15%	222	429	51.75%	53.46%
NDX	Higher high 4 days in a row		1 week	0.10%	0.37%	232	429	54.08%	56.36%
NDX	Higher high 5 days in a row		1 day	0.03%	0.08%	140	255	54.90%	54.14%
NDX	Higher high 5 days in a row		2 days	-0.03%	0.15%	132	255	51.76%	53.46%
NDX	Higher high 5 days in a row		1 week	0.20%	0.37%	140	255	54.90%	56.36%
NDX	Lower low 3 days in a row		1 day	0.23%	0.08%	285	483	59.01%	54.14%
NDX	Lower low 3 days in a row		2 days	0.32%	0.15%	269	485	55.46%	53.46%
NDX	Lower low 3 days in a row		1 week	0.94%	0.37%	290	485	59.79%	56.36%
NDX	Lower low 4 days in a row		1 day	0.43%	0.08%	149	248	60.08%	54.14%
NDX	Lower low 4 days in a row		2 days	0.61%	0.15%	143	248	57.66%	53.46%
NDX	Lower low 4 days in a row		1 week	1.28%	0.37%	152	248	61.29%	56.36%
NDX	Lower low 5 days in a row		1 day	0.71%	0.08%	80	127	62.99%	54.14%
NDX	Lower low 5 days in a row		2 days	0.97%	0.15%	81	127	63.78%	53.46%
NDX	Lower low 5 days in a row		1 week	1.59%	0.37%	79	127	62.20%	56.36%
NDX	Higher high 3 days in a row	Above 200-day MA	1 day	0.08%	0.09%	335	608	55.10%	54.96%
NDX	Higher high 3 days in a row	Above 200-day MA	2 days	0.13%	0.19%	327	606	53.96%	54.80%
NDX	Higher high 3 days in a row	Above 200-day MA	1 week	0.21%	0.49%	338	607	55.68%	58.40%
NDX	Higher high 4 days in a row	Above 200-day MA	1 day	0.05%	0.09%	203	374	54.28%	54.96%
NDX	Higher high 4 days in a row	Above 200-day MA	2 days	0.09%	0.19%	200	374	53.48%	54.80%
NDX	Higher high 4 days in a row	Above 200-day MA	1 week	0.28%	0.49%	208	374	55.61%	58.40%
NDX	Higher high 5 days in a row	Above 200-day MA	1 day	0.08%	0.09%	132	232	56.90%	54.96%
NDX	Higher high 5 days in a row	Above 200-day MA	2 days	0.12%	0.19%	126	232	54.31%	54.80%
NDX	Higher high 5 days in a row	Above 200-day MA	1 week	0.40%	0.49%	132	232	56.90%	58.40%
NDX	Lower low 3 days in a row	Above 200-day MA	1 day	0.27%	0.09%	164	262	62.60%	54.96%
NDX	Lower low 3 days in a row	Above 200-day MA	2 days	0.52%	0.19%	156	262	59.54%	54.80%
NDX	Lower low 3 days in a row	Above 200-day MA	1 week	1.19%	0.49%	170	262	64.89%	58.40%
NDX	Lower low 4 days in a row	Above 200-day MA	1 day	0.46%	0.09%	76	118	64.41%	54.96%
NDX	Lower low 4 days in a row	Above 200-day MA	2 days	0.81%	0.19%	74	118	62.71%	54.80%
NDX	Lower low 4 days in a row	Above 200-day MA	1 week	1.39%	0.49%	79	118	66.95%	58.40%
NDX	Lower low 5 days in a row	Above 200-day MA	1 day	0.81%	0.09%	40	58	68.97%	54.96%
NDX	Lower low 5 days in a row	Above 200-day MA	2 days	1.16%	0.19%	42	58	72.41%	54.80%
NDX	Lower low 5 days in a row	Above 200-day MA	1 week	1.43%	0.49%	40	58	68.97%	58.40%
NDX	Higher high 3 days in a row	Below 200-day MA	1 day	-0.05%	0.03%	57	116	49.14%	52.03%
NDX	Higher high 3 days in a row	Below 200-day MA	2 days	-0.16%	0.04%	54	116	46.55%	49.91%
NDX	Higher high 3 days in a row	Below 200-day MA	1 week	-0.33%	0.06%	58	116	50.00%	51.13%
NDX	Higher high 4 days in a row	Below 200-day MA	1 day	-0.31%	0.03%	25	55	45.45%	52.03%
NDX	Higher high 4 days in a row	Below 200-day MA	2 days	-0.76%	0.04%	22	55	40.00%	49.91%
NDX	Higher high 4 days in a row	Below 200-day MA	1 week	-1.14%	0.06%	24	55	43.64%	51.13%
NDX	Higher high 5 days in a row	Below 200-day MA	1 day	-0.57%	0.03%	8	23	34.78%	52.03%
NDX	Higher high 5 days in a row	Below 200-day MA	2 days	-1.57%	0.04%	6	23	26.09%	49.91%
NDX	Higher high 5 days in a row	Below 200-day MA	1 week	-1.85%	0.06%	8	23	34.78%	51.13%
NDX	Lower low 3 days in a row	Below 200-day MA	1 day	0.19%	0.03%	121	221	54.75%	52.03%
NDX	Lower low 3 days in a row	Below 200-day MA	2 days	0.08%	0.04%	113	223	50.67%	49.91%
NDX	Lower low 3 days in a row	Below 200-day MA	1 week	0.64%	0.06%	120	223	53.81%	51.13%
NDX	Lower low 4 days in a row	Below 200-day MA	1 day	0.40%	0.03%	73	130	56.15%	52.03%
NDX	Lower low 4 days in a row	Below 200-day MA	2 days	0.43%	0.04%	69	130	53.08%	49.91%
NDX	Lower low 4 days in a row	Below 200-day MA	1 week	1.18%	0.06%	73	130	56.15%	51.13%
NDX	Lower low 5 days in a row	Below 200-day MA	1 day	0.62%	0.03%	40	69	57.97%	52.03%
NDX	Lower low 5 days in a row	Below 200-day MA	2 days	0.81%	0.04%	39	69	56.52%	49.91%
NDX	Lower low 5 days in a row	Below 200-day MA	1 week	1.72%	0.06%	39	69	56.52%	51.13%

SUMMARY AND CONCLUSION

At the beginning of this chapter we asked, "Is it better to be a buyer after the market has been strong and has made multiple days of higher highs? And, is it better to be a seller after the market has shown signs of weakness and has made multiple days of lower lows?" **The answer (to both) is a resounding "no."**

As you can see, the greater opportunity and edge has been from being a buyer as the market has made lower lows versus buying when it makes higher highs. Why is this so? It is for the same reasons we mentioned in the previous chapter. It's likely because a market usually makes a new high "after" good news has occurred. This good news could be a slew of positive economic reports, positive earnings, etc. The buying has "already occurred." On the opposite side, new lows are usually accompanied by bad economic news, bad earnings, etc. The sellers have taken prices lower and from there the buyers get to step in, especially those correctly anticipating better news in the near future.

Now let's look at when markets rise and fall consecutive days in a row.

CHAPTER 4

UP DAYS IN A ROW vs. DOWN DAYS IN A ROW

What does the market do after it rises or falls consecutive days in a row?

Common wisdom states that a market that rallies a few days in a row is strong and a market that drops a few days in a row is weak.

A summary of our findings is as follows:

Returns Increased Following Consecutive Days of Market Declines; Returns Decreased Following Consecutive Days of Market Gains

1. After the SPX has risen 2 days in a row (and 3 days in a row), the market has underperformed the benchmark over the next 2 days and also over the next week. When the SPX declined 2 days in a row (and 3 days in a row), the market has proceeded to outperform the benchmark over the next 2 days and the next week.

Consecutive Days of Declining Markets Far Outperformed Consecutive Days of Rising Markets

2. When comparing 2 days up in a row to 2 days down in a row, the difference in the returns is significant. After the SPX has dropped 2 days in a row, it has risen on average .48% after one week. When it has rallied 2 days in a row, it has risen only .07% over the next week. The edge in 3 days is row is even more significant. After the SPX has dropped 3 days in row the market has risen on average .84% over the next week. When it has risen 3 days in row, the average gains were just .04% over the following one-week period.

Nasdaq Mirrored S&P Results When Looking at Multiple Days Higher and Multiple Days Lower

3. When we look at the NDX we see basically the same trend. Both 2 and 3 up days in a row underperform 2 and 3 down days in a row.

Consecutive Days of Market Gains in a Downtrend Led to Negative Returns

4. Another interesting finding is how the SPX and the NDX *lost* money after one week when rising 2 and 3 days in a row in a down trending market (under the 200-day moving average). This information is especially useful for traders who look to short the market when it's in a decline.

There is obviously an abundance of information that can be gleaned from this chapter and we encourage you to spend time with the numbers. The results we found were further confirmed when we studied the period from 1974–1988 and ran the same tests. Looking back at a total of 30 years on this one aspect of price behavior provided us with the same conclusions as looking at the test for 15 years.

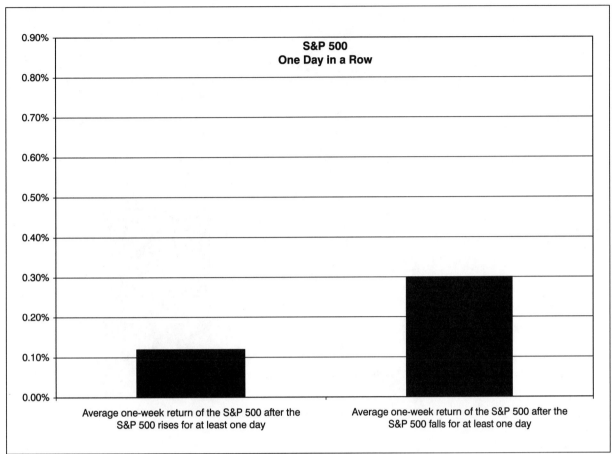

Figure 4-1   1989–2003

*Down Days Have Slightly Outperformed Up Days After 1 Week. Said
Another Way, Over the Next Week, it Was Better for the Market to Have
Dropped Today.*

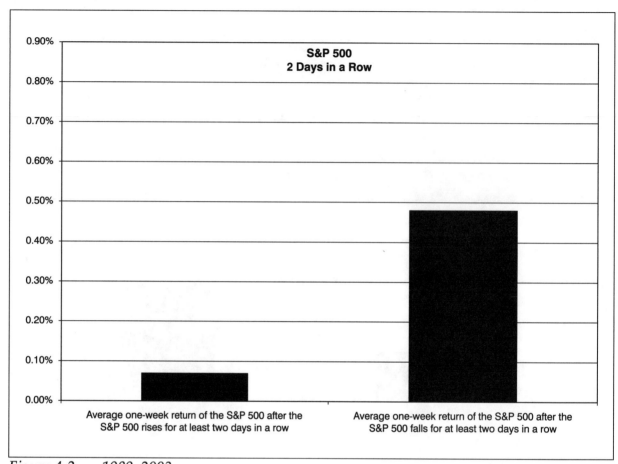

Figure 4-2   1989–2003

2 Down Days in a Row Outperformed 2 Up Days in a Row After 1 Week

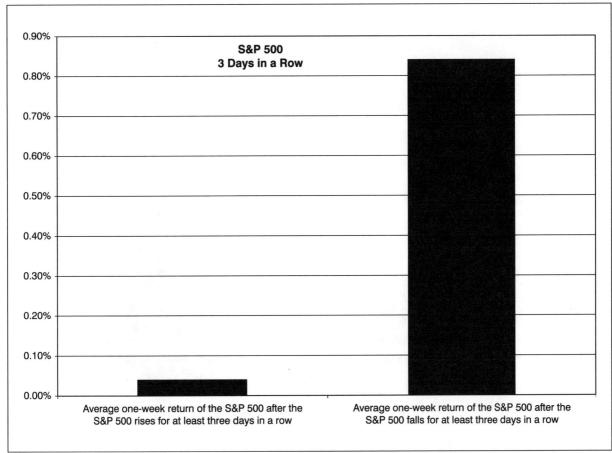

Figure 4-3   *1989–2003*

3 Down Days in a Row Vastly Outperformed 3 Up Days in a Row After 1 Week

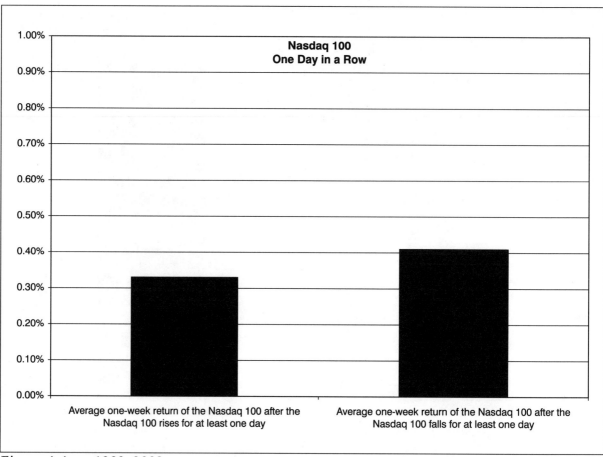

Figure 4-4   1989–2003

An Up Day in the Nasdaq Has Slightly Underperformed a Down Day in the Nasdaq After 1 Week

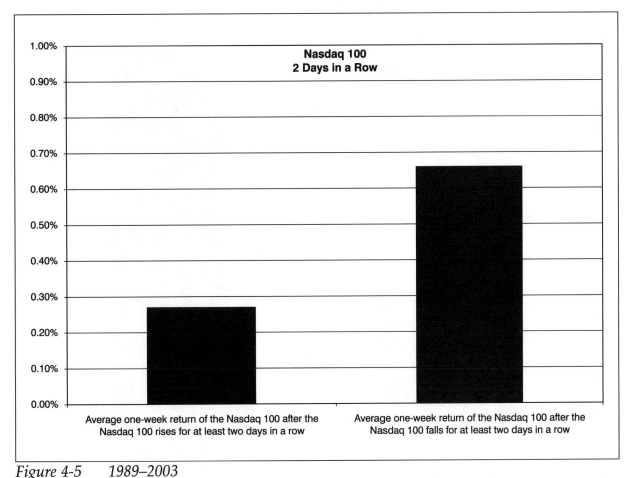

Figure 4-5   1989–2003

2 Down Days in a Row in the Nasdaq Outperformed 2 Up Days in a Row After 1 Week

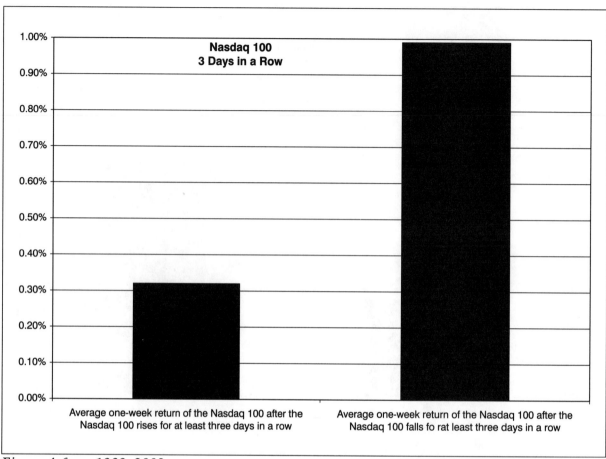

Figure 4-6   1989–2003

3 Down Days in a Row Have Outperformed 3 Up Days in a Row in the Nasdaq by an Almost 3-1 Margin After 1 Week

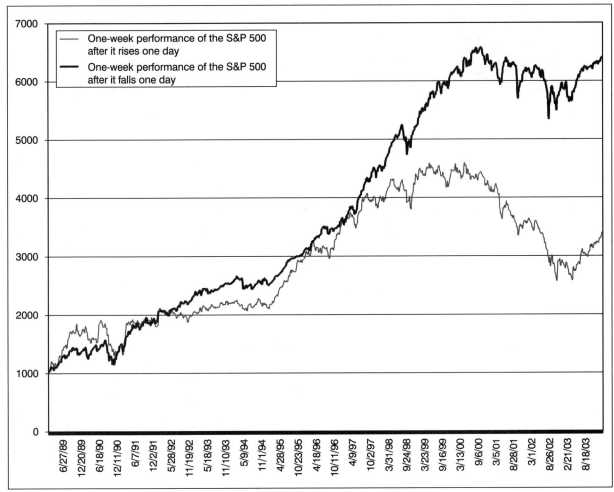

Figure 4-7

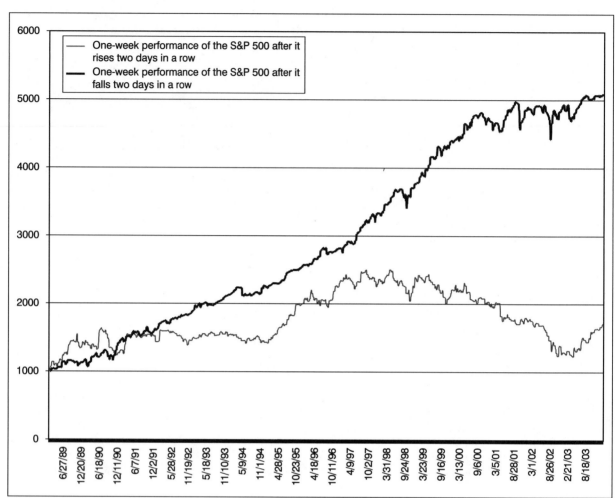

Figure 4-8

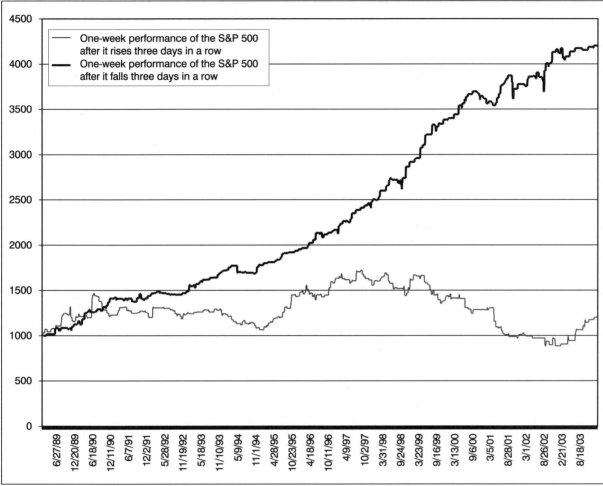

Figure 4-9

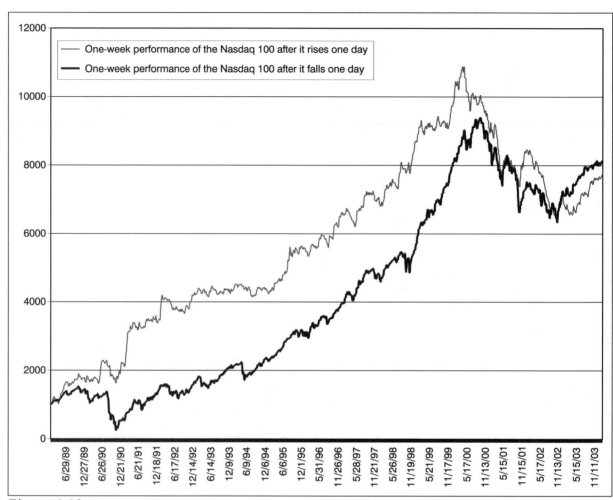

Figure 4-10

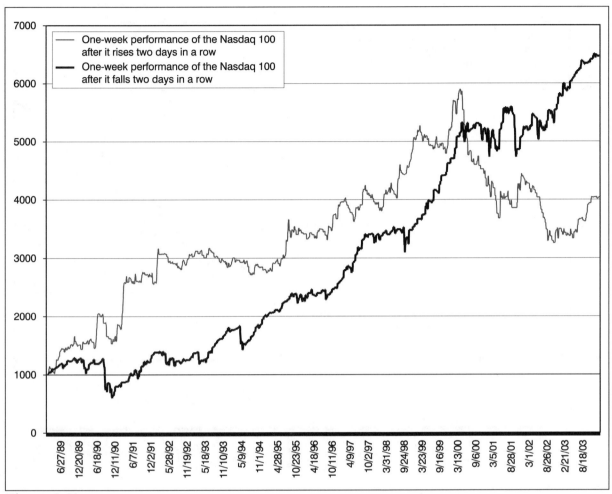

Figure 4-11

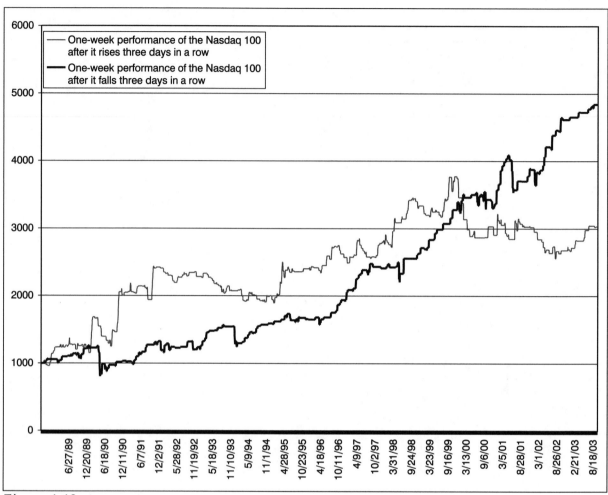

Figure 4-12

Index	Rule 1	Rule 2	Time Period	Gain/Loss	Benchmark Avg	# Winners	# Days	% Profitable	% Profitable Benchmark
SPX	After 1 up day		1 day	0.06%	0.04%	1053	1991	52.89%	52.71%
SPX	After 1 up day		2 days	0.08%	0.08%	1092	1990	54.87%	54.11%
SPX	After 1 up day		1 week	0.12%	0.21%	1123	1989	56.46%	56.66%
SPX	After 2 up days		1 day	0.06%	0.04%	545	1051	51.86%	52.71%
SPX	After 2 up days		2 days	0.06%	0.08%	576	1050	54.86%	54.11%
SPX	After 2 up days		1 week	0.07%	0.21%	599	1050	57.05%	56.66%
SPX	After 3 up days		1 day	0.03%	0.04%	267	544	49.08%	52.71%
SPX	After 3 up days		2 days	-0.01%	0.08%	287	543	52.85%	54.11%
SPX	After 3 up days		1 week	0.04%	0.21%	320	543	58.93%	56.66%
SPX	After 1 down day		1 day	0.02%	0.04%	939	1788	52.52%	52.71%
SPX	After 1 down day		2 days	0.08%	0.08%	952	1787	53.27%	54.11%
SPX	After 1 down day		1 week	0.30%	0.21%	1016	1788	56.82%	56.66%
SPX	After 2 down days		1 day	0.07%	0.04%	467	848	55.07%	52.71%
SPX	After 2 down days		2 days	0.18%	0.08%	462	848	54.48%	54.11%
SPX	After 2 down days		1 week	0.48%	0.21%	498	849	58.66%	56.66%
SPX	After 3 down days		1 day	0.17%	0.04%	229	380	60.26%	52.71%
SPX	After 3 down days		2 days	0.35%	0.08%	223	380	58.68%	54.11%
SPX	After 3 down days		1 week	0.84%	0.21%	242	381	63.52%	56.66%
SPX	After 1 up day	Above 200-day MA	1 day	0.08%	0.05%	816	1514	53.90%	53.49%
SPX	After 1 up day	Above 200-day MA	2 days	0.13%	0.10%	861	1513	56.91%	55.56%
SPX	After 1 up day	Above 200-day MA	1 week	0.18%	0.25%	878	1512	58.07%	58.22%
SPX	After 2 up days	Above 200-day MA	1 day	0.07%	0.05%	438	835	52.46%	53.49%
SPX	After 2 up days	Above 200-day MA	2 days	0.11%	0.10%	470	834	56.35%	55.56%
SPX	After 2 up days	Above 200-day MA	1 week	0.12%	0.25%	484	834	58.03%	58.22%
SPX	After 3 up days	Above 200-day MA	1 day	0.05%	0.05%	223	449	49.67%	53.49%
SPX	After 3 up days	Above 200-day MA	2 days	0.06%	0.10%	243	448	54.24%	55.56%
SPX	After 3 up days	Above 200-day MA	1 week	0.07%	0.25%	263	448	58.71%	58.22%
SPX	After 1 down day	Above 200-day MA	1 day	0.02%	0.05%	655	1236	52.99%	53.49%
SPX	After 1 down day	Above 200-day MA	2 days	0.07%	0.10%	666	1235	53.93%	55.56%
SPX	After 1 down day	Above 200-day MA	1 week	0.33%	0.25%	721	1236	58.33%	58.22%
SPX	After 2 down days	Above 200-day MA	1 day	0.01%	0.05%	305	555	54.95%	53.49%
SPX	After 2 down days	Above 200-day MA	2 days	0.14%	0.10%	310	555	55.86%	55.56%
SPX	After 2 down days	Above 200-day MA	1 week	0.47%	0.25%	333	556	59.89%	58.22%
SPX	After 3 down days	Above 200-day MA	1 day	0.13%	0.05%	146	235	62.13%	53.49%
SPX	After 3 down days	Above 200-day MA	2 days	0.36%	0.10%	142	235	60.43%	55.56%
SPX	After 3 down days	Above 200-day MA	1 week	0.80%	0.25%	156	236	66.10%	58.22%
SPX	After 1 up day	Below 200-day MA	1 day	0.01%	0.02%	237	477	49.69%	50.63%
SPX	After 1 up day	Below 200-day MA	2 days	-0.06%	0.04%	231	477	48.43%	50.24%
SPX	After 1 up day	Below 200-day MA	1 week	-0.08%	0.09%	245	477	51.36%	52.48%
SPX	After 2 up days	Below 200-day MA	1 day	0.03%	0.02%	107	216	49.54%	50.63%
SPX	After 2 up days	Below 200-day MA	2 days	-0.14%	0.04%	106	216	49.07%	50.24%
SPX	After 2 up days	Below 200-day MA	1 week	-0.12%	0.09%	115	216	53.24%	52.48%
SPX	After 3 up days	Below 200-day MA	1 day	-0.07%	0.02%	44	95	46.32%	50.63%
SPX	After 3 up days	Below 200-day MA	2 days	-0.36%	0.04%	44	95	46.32%	50.24%
SPX	After 3 up days	Below 200-day MA	1 week	-0.12%	0.09%	57	95	60.00%	52.48%
SPX	After 1 down day	Below 200-day MA	1 day	0.03%	0.02%	284	552	51.45%	50.63%
SPX	After 1 down day	Below 200-day MA	2 days	0.12%	0.04%	286	552	51.81%	50.24%
SPX	After 1 down day	Below 200-day MA	1 week	0.24%	0.09%	295	552	53.44%	52.48%
SPX	After 2 down days	Below 200-day MA	1 day	0.16%	0.02%	162	293	55.29%	50.63%
SPX	After 2 down days	Below 200-day MA	2 days	0.27%	0.04%	152	293	51.88%	50.24%
SPX	After 2 down days	Below 200-day MA	1 week	0.51%	0.09%	165	293	56.31%	52.48%
SPX	After 3 down days	Below 200-day MA	1 day	0.23%	0.02%	83	145	57.24%	50.63%
SPX	After 3 down days	Below 200-day MA	2 days	0.35%	0.04%	81	145	55.86%	50.24%
SPX	After 3 down days	Below 200-day MA	1 week	0.91%	0.09%	86	145	59.31%	52.48%

See page 17 for column descriptions.

Index	Rule 1	Rule 2	Time Period	Gain/Loss	Benchmark Avg	# Winners	# Days	% Profitable	% Profitable Benchmark
NDX	After 1 up day		1 day	0.13%	0.08%	1146	2041	56.15%	54.14%
NDX	After 1 up day		2 days	0.14%	0.15%	1116	2044	54.60%	53.43%
NDX	After 1 up day		1 week	0.33%	0.37%	1160	2043	56.78%	56.36%
NDX	After 2 up days		1 day	0.09%	0.08%	634	1143	55.47%	54.14%
NDX	After 2 up days		2 days	0.09%	0.15%	622	1146	54.28%	53.43%
NDX	After 2 up days		1 week	0.27%	0.37%	649	1145	56.68%	56.36%
NDX	After 3 up days		1 day	0.08%	0.08%	350	633	55.29%	54.14%
NDX	After 3 up days		2 days	0.08%	0.15%	335	634	52.84%	53.43%
NDX	After 3 up days		1 week	0.32%	0.37%	361	634	56.94%	56.36%
NDX	After 1 down day		1 day	0.01%	0.08%	897	1730	51.85%	54.14%
NDX	After 1 down day		2 days	0.17%	0.15%	902	1731	52.11%	53.43%
NDX	After 1 down day		1 week	0.41%	0.37%	967	1730	55.90%	56.36%
NDX	After 2 down days		1 day	0.13%	0.08%	443	830	53.37%	54.14%
NDX	After 2 down days		2 days	0.35%	0.15%	448	832	53.85%	53.43%
NDX	After 2 down days		1 week	0.66%	0.37%	478	832	57.45%	56.36%
NDX	After 3 down days		1 day	0.38%	0.08%	217	385	56.36%	54.14%
NDX	After 3 down days		2 days	0.59%	0.15%	224	387	57.88%	53.43%
NDX	After 3 down days		1 week	0.99%	0.37%	237	387	61.24%	56.36%
NDX	After 1 up day	Above 200-day MA	1 day	0.14%	0.11%	874	1541	56.72%	54.96%
NDX	After 1 up day	Above 200-day MA	2 days	0.20%	0.15%	865	1543	56.06%	54.80%
NDX	After 1 up day	Above 200-day MA	1 week	0.48%	0.30%	912	1542	59.14%	58.40%
NDX	After 2 up days	Above 200-day MA	1 day	0.08%	0.11%	500	898	55.68%	54.96%
NDX	After 2 up days	Above 200-day MA	2 days	0.16%	0.15%	498	901	55.27%	54.80%
NDX	After 2 up days	Above 200-day MA	1 week	0.40%	0.30%	527	900	58.56%	58.40%
NDX	After 3 up days	Above 200-day MA	1 day	0.09%	0.11%	286	509	56.19%	54.96%
NDX	After 3 up days	Above 200-day MA	2 days	0.15%	0.15%	273	510	53.53%	54.80%
NDX	After 3 up days	Above 200-day MA	1 week	0.41%	0.30%	300	510	58.82%	58.40%
NDX	After 1 down day	Above 200-day MA	1 day	0.03%	0.11%	620	1176	52.72%	54.96%
NDX	After 1 down day	Above 200-day MA	2 days	0.18%	0.15%	625	1175	53.19%	54.80%
NDX	After 1 down day	Above 200-day MA	1 week	0.49%	0.30%	674	1174	57.41%	58.40%
NDX	After 2 down days	Above 200-day MA	1 day	0.07%	0.11%	283	529	53.50%	54.96%
NDX	After 2 down days	Above 200-day MA	2 days	0.33%	0.15%	291	529	55.01%	54.80%
NDX	After 2 down days	Above 200-day MA	1 week	0.57%	0.30%	304	529	57.47%	58.40%
NDX	After 3 down days	Above 200-day MA	1 day	0.25%	0.11%	131	231	56.71%	54.96%
NDX	After 3 down days	Above 200-day MA	2 days	0.59%	0.15%	137	231	59.31%	54.80%
NDX	After 3 down days	Above 200-day MA	1 week	0.65%	0.30%	139	231	60.17%	58.40%
NDX	After 1 up day	Below 200-day MA	1 day	0.10%	0.03%	272	500	54.40%	52.03%
NDX	After 1 up day	Below 200-day MA	2 days	-0.06%	0.04%	251	501	50.10%	49.91%
NDX	After 1 up day	Below 200-day MA	1 week	-0.14%	0.06%	248	501	49.50%	51.13%
NDX	After 2 up days	Below 200-day MA	1 day	0.10%	0.03%	134	245	54.69%	52.03%
NDX	After 2 up days	Below 200-day MA	2 days	-0.15%	0.04%	124	245	50.61%	49.91%
NDX	After 2 up days	Below 200-day MA	1 week	-0.22%	0.06%	122	245	49.80%	51.13%
NDX	After 3 up days	Below 200-day MA	1 day	0.01%	0.03%	64	124	51.61%	52.03%
NDX	After 3 up days	Below 200-day MA	2 days	-0.23%	0.04%	62	124	50.00%	49.91%
NDX	After 3 up days	Below 200-day MA	1 week	-0.05%	0.06%	61	124	49.19%	51.13%
NDX	After 1 down day	Below 200-day MA	1 day	-0.22%	0.03%	277	554	50.00%	52.03%
NDX	After 1 down day	Below 200-day MA	2 days	0.15%	0.04%	277	556	49.82%	49.91%
NDX	After 1 down day	Below 200-day MA	1 week	0.24%	0.06%	293	556	52.70%	51.13%
NDX	After 2 down days	Below 200-day MA	1 day	0.24%	0.03%	160	301	53.16%	52.03%
NDX	After 2 down days	Below 200-day MA	2 days	0.40%	0.04%	157	303	51.82%	49.91%
NDX	After 2 down days	Below 200-day MA	1 week	0.81%	0.06%	174	303	57.43%	51.13%
NDX	After 3 down days	Below 200-day MA	1 day	0.57%	0.03%	86	154	55.84%	52.03%
NDX	After 3 down days	Below 200-day MA	2 days	0.60%	0.04%	87	156	55.77%	49.91%
NDX	After 3 down days	Below 200-day MA	1 week	1.50%	0.06%	98	156	62.82%	51.13%

SUMMARY AND CONCLUSION

Our test results show that there has been an edge on the long side when the market has *declined* multiple days in a row instead of rising multiple days in a row. The notion that short-term market strength follows through with more strength again appears to be wrong. In fact, the results show fairly conclusively that short-term weakness is followed by short-term strength and short-term strength is followed by short-term underperformance. This again leads to the conclusion that, should these result continue to hold true in the future, waiting for a market to decline multiple days in a row is better than buying into strength.

Let's now look at how the market has performed during extreme levels of daily advancing and declining issues.

CHAPTER 5

MARKET BREADTH

Nearly every night of the business week the financial press reports the number of stocks that have advanced versus the number of stocks that have declined for the day. "Advancing issues led declining issues by a 2-1 margin." "Declining issues outnumbered advancing issues 2076 to 1103." And, usually the bigger the difference in the two numbers, the more likely you will hear adjectives used such as "healthy" to describe the good days and "poor" to describe the days that declining issues far outnumber the advancing issues. On the days that the numbers are truly far apart, you'll undoubtedly hear analysts telling you just how good things are because so many more stocks rose for the day and they'll tell you just how weak things look when so many more stocks declined for the day.

This type of analysis seems logical, doesn't it? More stocks rising supposedly means strong market breadth and a broad-based rally. And more stocks declining in price for the day means weakness. And, supposedly this weakness is a bad sign. This attitude and interpretation of daily price movement is amongst the most prevalent thought processes found on Wall Street.

We looked at an 8-year period from 1996–2003. The market over that time rose strongly, then declined sharply and then recovered in 2003. It saw both bull moves and a bear move. We looked at market breadth two distinct ways. First we looked at advancing issues being greater than declining issues for multiple days in a row. Conventional wisdom is that the more days advancing issues exceed declining issues, the stronger the market internals are. The opposite is true for when declining issues exceed advancing issues for a number of days. When this occurs, the market is showing weakness and this weakness is interpreted as negative for the near future.

Our second test looked at the days when advancing issues outnumbered declining issues by a 2-1 margin and a 3-1 margin. When this happens, it means the rally is broad based and analysts usually tell you it's a very healthy sign. The opposite occurs when declining issues outnumber advancing issues by a 2-1 and 3-1 margin. Reportedly, things are bleak and it's interpreted as a bad sign.

Let's now look at the results. As you will see the results are clear-cut.

Consecutive Days of Declining Issues Greater Than Advancing Issues on the NYSE Has Led to Higher Prices Short-Term

1. The first thing that is apparent is that multiple days of declining issues greater than advancing issues for both the SPX and the NDX not only outperformed the benchmark over the next week, but they also far outperformed the times when there were multiple days of advancing issues greater than declining issues. For example, look at the NDX when declining issues outnumbered advancing issues 2 days in a row. Over the next week, the average gain was .81%. When advancing issues were greater than declining issues 2 days in a row in the NDX, the market *lost* .23% over the next week. We see the same type of results for 3 days and we see the same type of results in the SPX. There is a consistent theme here . . . multiple days of declining issues being greater than advancing issues is not a sign of future weakness. It's a sign that a rally is likely near and at least over the 8 years tested, this rally has been stronger than average.

Significant Underperformance Occurs When Advancing Issues Outnumber Declining Issues and the Market Is Trading Under Its 200-day Moving Average

2. When you look at advancing issues greater than declining issues when the market is under its 200-day moving average, the results become even more obvious. Some of the losses during this time are significant and underperform the average 1-week hold even further.

Poor Breadth Days Outperformed Strong Breadth Days

3. We then looked at the times when advancing issues outnumbered declining issues by a 2-1 margin and a 3-1 margin. These are the times when the market is supposedly "strong and healthy." Again, the results show this not to be true. When advancing issues outnumber declining issues by a 2-1 margin, the market lost money over the next week for both the SPX and the NDX (again, in spite of an upward bias in prices). The negative returns are also seen over the next week in the NDX. When declining issues outnumbered advancing issues by a 2-1 and 3-1 margin, the following week has seen gains as the market, on average, rose. And, when you match things up, it's obvious that at least from 1996-2003, you would have been better off being a buyer after these supposedly bad days versus being a buyer when breadth was strong.

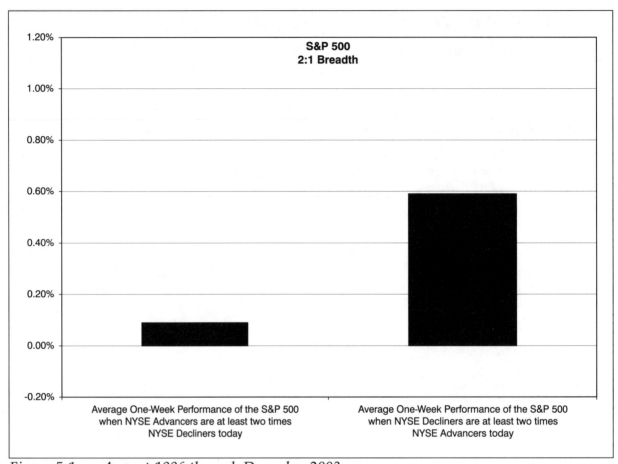

Figure 5-1   August 1996 through December 2003

Days with 2:1 Decliners Outperformed Days with 2:1 Advancers

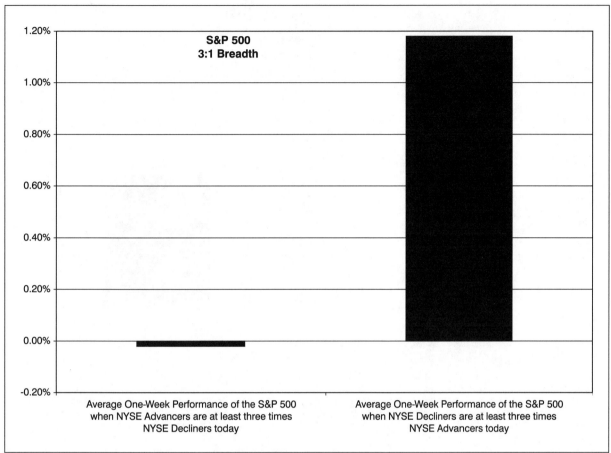

Figure 5-2   August 1996 through December 2003

The Market (on Average) Has Lost Money Within a Week Following Days When Advancing Issues Outnumbered Declining Issues by at Least 3:1

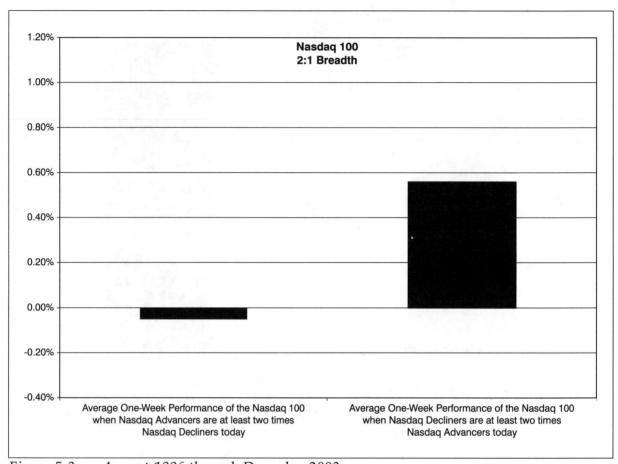

Figure 5-3   August 1996 through December 2003

Weak Nasdaq Breadth Has Outperformed Strong Nasdaq Breadth After 1 Week

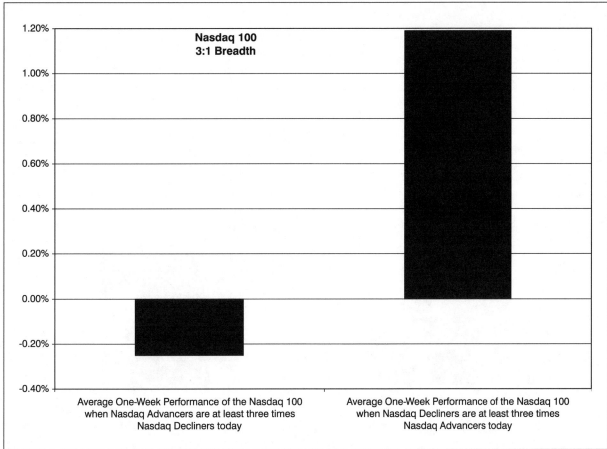

Figure 5-4   August 1996 through December 2003

When the Nasdaq Declining Issues Outnumbered Advancing Issues by a 3:1 Margin, Strong Performance Has Followed. When the Advancing Issues Outnumbered Declining Issues by a 3:1 Margin, the Nasdaq (on Average) Has Lost Money

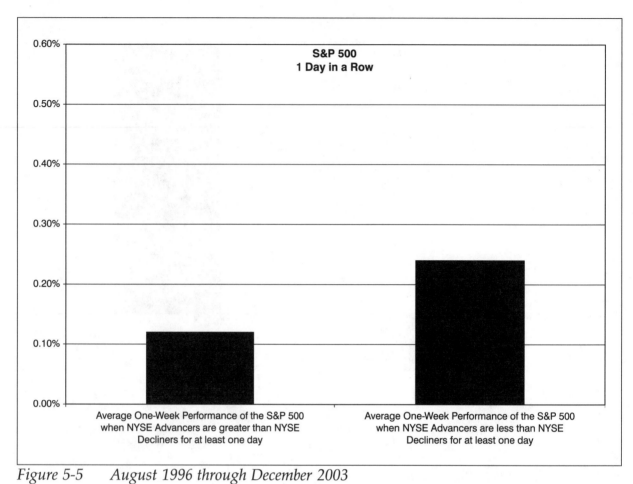

Figure 5-5   August 1996 through December 2003

Declining Issues Outnumbering Advancing Issues Has Led to a Small Outperformance Over the Next Week

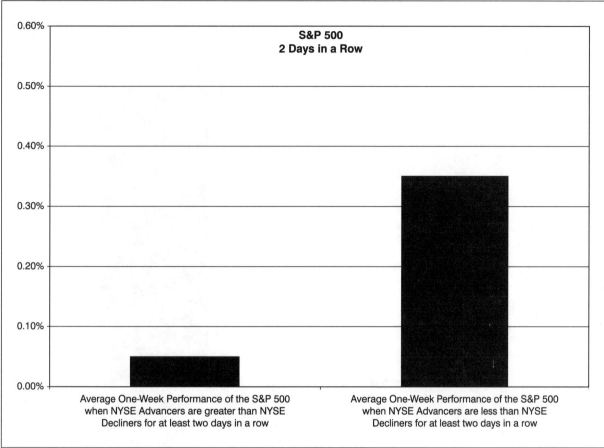

Figure 5-6   August 1996 through December 2003

2 Consecutive Days of Declining Issues Outnumbering Advancing Issues Has Outperformed 2 Consecutive Days of Advancing Issues Outnumbering Declining Issues

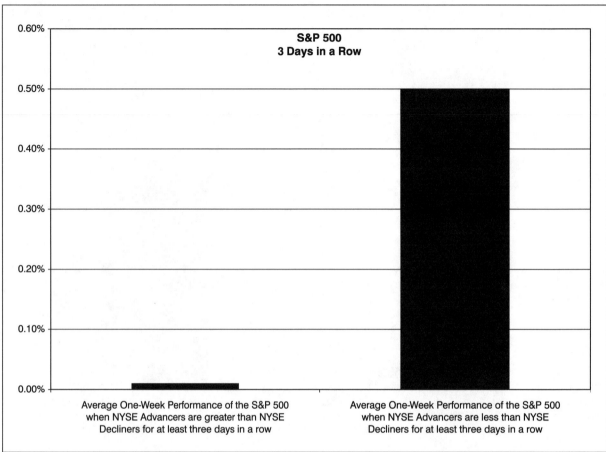

Figure 5-7   *August 1996 through December 2003*

3 Consecutive Days of Declining Issues Greater Than Advancing Issues Have Strongly Outperformed 3 Consecutive Days of Advancing Issues Greater Than Declining Issues

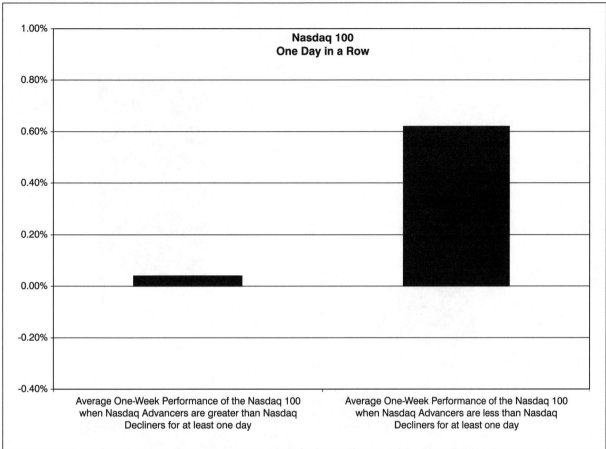

Figure 5-8   August 1996 through December 2003

Days with Declining Issues Outnumbering Advancing Issues in the Nasdaq Have Outperformed Days with Advancing Issues Outnumbering Declining Issues

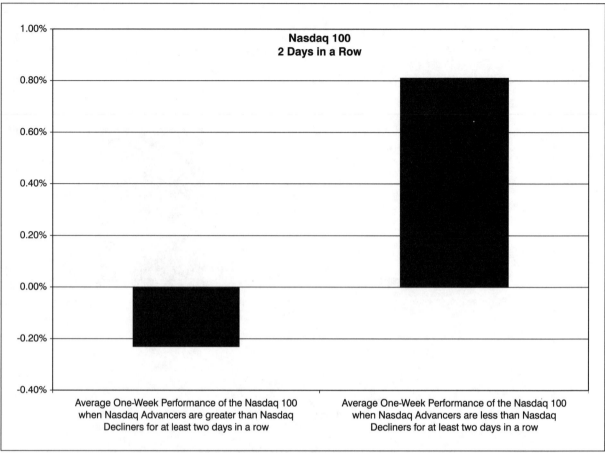

Figure 5-9   *August 1996 through December 2003*

2 Days in a Row of Declining Issues Greater Than Advancing Issues in the Nasdaq Significantly Outperformed 2 Days in a Row of Advancing Issues Greater Than Declining Issues

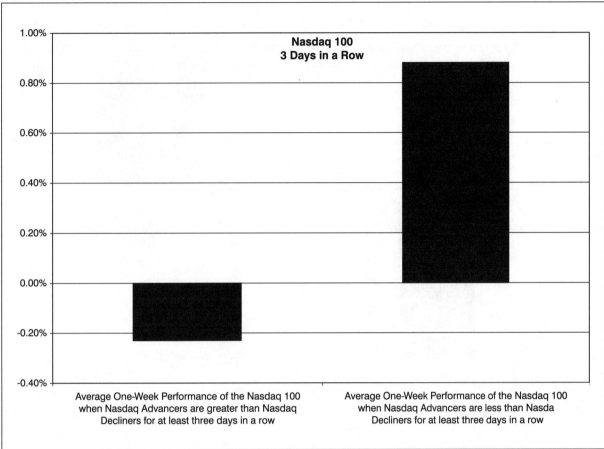

Figure 5-10   August 1996 through December 2003

3 Consecutive Days of Advancing Issues Outnumbering Declining Issues Has Led (on Average) to Losses Over the Next Week for the Nasdaq

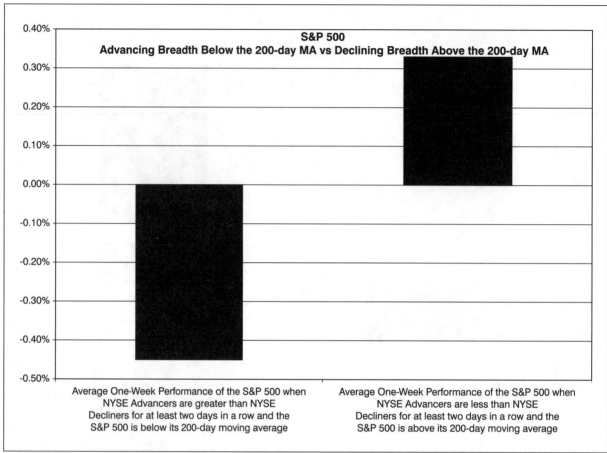

Figure 5-11   *August 1996 through December 2003*

The S&P Has Seen Declines the Week Following 2 Days of Advancers Greater Than Decliners When Under Its 200-Day Moving Average

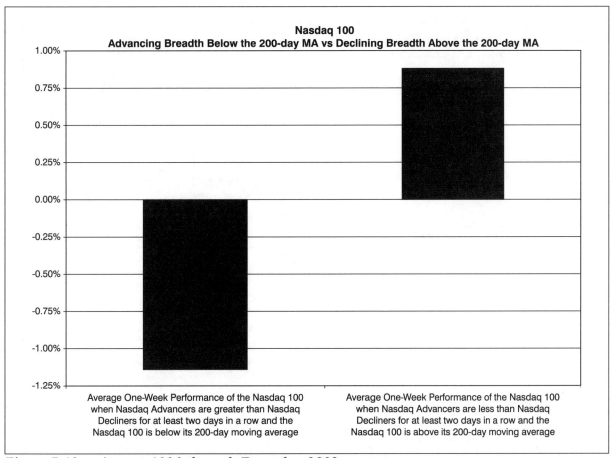

Figure 5-12   August 1996 through December 2003

Trend Combined with Breadth Has Made a Good Combination

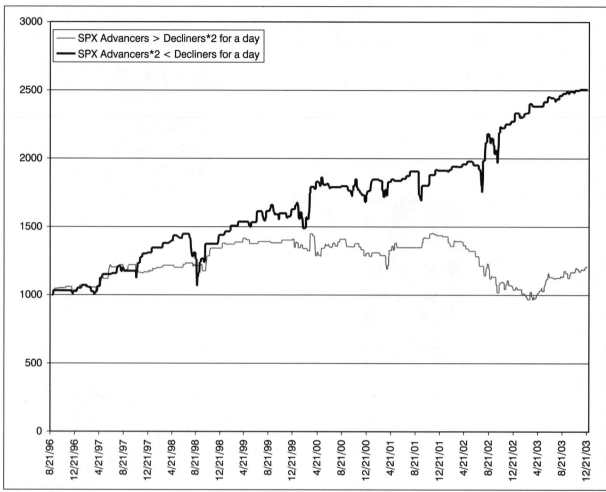

Figure 5-13

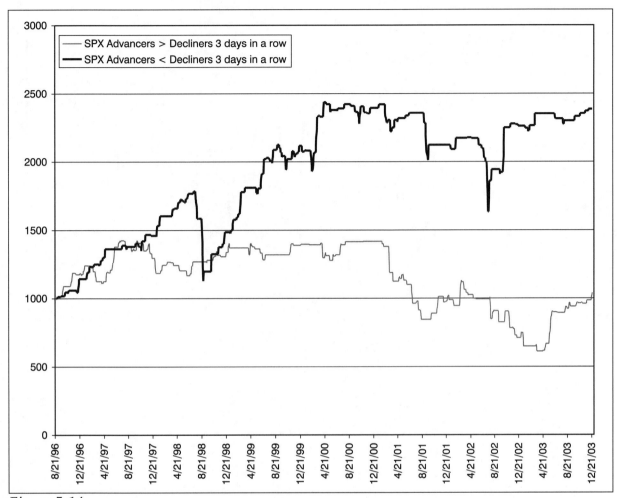

Figure 5-14

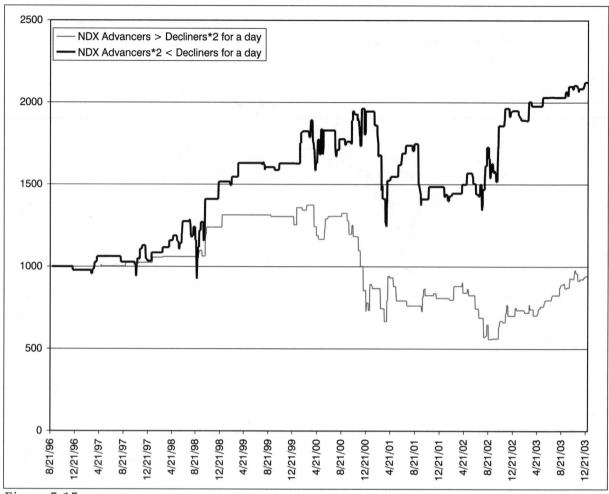

Figure 5-15

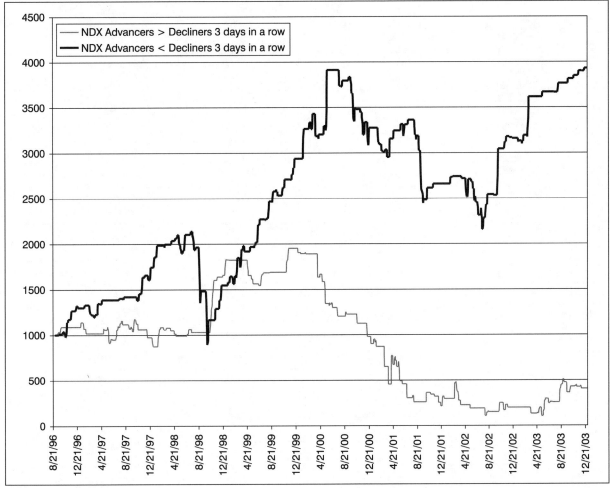

Figure 5-16

Index	Rule 1	Rule 2	Time Period	Gain/Loss	Benchmark Avg	# Winners	# Days	% Profitable	% Profitable Benchmark
SPX	Adv > 2*Dec for one day		1 day	-0.01%	0.04%	119	235	50.64%	51.20%
SPX	Adv > 2*Dec for one day		2 days	-0.05%	0.07%	119	235	50.64%	53.50%
SPX	Adv > 2*Dec for one day		1 week	0.09%	0.17%	126	235	53.62%	54.30%
SPX	Adv > 3*Dec for one day		1 day	-0.16%	0.04%	27	59	45.76%	51.20%
SPX	Adv > 3*Dec for one day		2 days	-0.11%	0.07%	28	59	47.46%	53.50%
SPX	Adv > 3*Dec for one day		1 week	-0.02%	0.17%	32	59	54.24%	54.30%
SPX	Adv*2 < Dec for one day		1 day	0.08%	0.04%	138	257	53.70%	51.20%
SPX	Adv*2 < Dec for one day		2 days	0.32%	0.07%	143	257	55.64%	53.50%
SPX	Adv*2 < Dec for one day		1 week	0.59%	0.17%	140	257	54.47%	54.30%
SPX	Adv*3 < Dec for one day		1 day	0.38%	0.04%	69	109	63.30%	51.20%
SPX	Adv*3 < Dec for one day		2 days	0.52%	0.07%	64	109	58.72%	53.50%
SPX	Adv*3 < Dec for one day		1 week	1.18%	0.17%	60	109	55.05%	54.30%
SPX	Adv > Dec 1 day in a row		1 day	0.07%	0.04%	492	954	51.57%	51.20%
SPX	Adv > Dec 1 day in a row		2 days	0.05%	0.07%	518	953	54.35%	53.50%
SPX	Adv > Dec 1 day in a row		1 week	0.12%	0.17%	517	950	54.42%	54.30%
SPX	Adv > Dec 2 days in a row		1 day	0.03%	0.04%	280	558	50.18%	51.20%
SPX	Adv > Dec 2 days in a row		2 days	0.05%	0.07%	312	557	56.01%	53.50%
SPX	Adv > Dec 2 days in a row		1 week	0.05%	0.17%	304	554	54.87%	54.30%
SPX	Adv > Dec 3 days in a row		1 day	0.08%	0.04%	173	327	52.91%	51.20%
SPX	Adv > Dec 3 days in a row		2 days	0.09%	0.07%	190	326	58.28%	53.50%
SPX	Adv > Dec 3 days in a row		1 week	0.01%	0.17%	180	323	55.73%	54.30%
SPX	Adv < Dec 1 day in a row		1 day	0.00%	0.04%	454	895	50.73%	51.20%
SPX	Adv < Dec 1 day in a row		2 days	0.10%	0.07%	470	896	52.46%	53.50%
SPX	Adv < Dec 1 day in a row		1 week	0.24%	0.17%	485	896	54.13%	54.30%
SPX	Adv < Dec 2 days in a row		1 day	0.08%	0.04%	270	498	54.22%	51.20%
SPX	Adv < Dec 2 days in a row		2 days	0.18%	0.07%	267	499	53.51%	53.50%
SPX	Adv < Dec 2 days in a row		1 week	0.35%	0.17%	277	499	55.51%	54.30%
SPX	Adv < Dec 3 days in a row		1 day	0.09%	0.04%	153	276	55.43%	51.20%
SPX	Adv < Dec 3 days in a row		2 days	0.18%	0.07%	147	277	53.07%	53.50%
SPX	Adv < Dec 3 days in a row		1 week	0.50%	0.17%	159	277	57.40%	54.30%
SPX	Adv > Dec 1 day in a row	Above 200-day MA	1 day	0.13%	0.05%	335	613	54.65%	52.80%
SPX	Adv > Dec 1 day in a row	Above 200-day MA	2 days	0.21%	0.12%	370	612	60.46%	56.40%
SPX	Adv > Dec 1 day in a row	Above 200-day MA	1 week	0.35%	0.30%	365	609	59.93%	57.80%
SPX	Adv > Dec 2 days in a row	Above 200-day MA	1 day	0.10%	0.05%	199	378	52.65%	52.80%
SPX	Adv > Dec 2 days in a row	Above 200-day MA	2 days	0.18%	0.12%	234	377	62.07%	56.40%
SPX	Adv > Dec 2 days in a row	Above 200-day MA	1 week	0.29%	0.30%	225	374	60.16%	57.80%
SPX	Adv > Dec 3 days in a row	Above 200-day MA	1 day	0.10%	0.05%	120	230	52.17%	52.80%
SPX	Adv > Dec 3 days in a row	Above 200-day MA	2 days	0.23%	0.12%	147	229	64.19%	56.40%
SPX	Adv > Dec 3 days in a row	Above 200-day MA	1 week	0.30%	0.30%	136	226	60.18%	57.80%
SPX	Adv < Dec 1 day in a row	Above 200-day MA	1 day	-0.03%	0.05%	275	543	50.64%	52.80%
SPX	Adv < Dec 1 day in a row	Above 200-day MA	2 days	0.02%	0.12%	282	544	51.84%	56.40%
SPX	Adv < Dec 1 day in a row	Above 200-day MA	1 week	0.25%	0.30%	302	544	55.51%	57.80%
SPX	Adv < Dec 2 days in a row	Above 200-day MA	1 day	-0.04%	0.05%	162	308	52.60%	52.80%
SPX	Adv < Dec 2 days in a row	Above 200-day MA	2 days	0.06%	0.12%	164	309	53.07%	56.40%
SPX	Adv < Dec 2 days in a row	Above 200-day MA	1 week	0.33%	0.30%	175	309	56.63%	57.80%
SPX	Adv < Dec 3 days in a row	Above 200-day MA	1 day	0.05%	0.05%	100	175	57.14%	52.80%
SPX	Adv < Dec 3 days in a row	Above 200-day MA	2 days	0.16%	0.12%	93	176	52.84%	56.40%
SPX	Adv < Dec 3 days in a row	Above 200-day MA	1 week	0.52%	0.30%	105	176	59.66%	57.80%
SPX	Adv > Dec 1 day in a row	Below 200-day MA	1 day	-0.05%	0.00%	157	341	46.04%	48.60%
SPX	Adv > Dec 1 day in a row	Below 200-day MA	2 days	-0.24%	-0.01%	148	341	43.40%	48.50%
SPX	Adv > Dec 1 day in a row	Below 200-day MA	1 week	-0.29%	-0.04%	152	341	44.57%	48.30%
SPX	Adv > Dec 2 days in a row	Below 200-day MA	1 day	-0.11%	0.00%	81	180	45.00%	48.60%
SPX	Adv > Dec 2 days in a row	Below 200-day MA	2 days	-0.22%	-0.01%	78	180	43.33%	48.50%
SPX	Adv > Dec 2 days in a row	Below 200-day MA	1 week	-0.45%	-0.04%	79	180	43.89%	48.30%
SPX	Adv > Dec 3 days in a row	Below 200-day MA	1 day	0.01%	0.00%	53	97	54.64%	48.60%
SPX	Adv > Dec 3 days in a row	Below 200-day MA	2 days	-0.23%	-0.01%	43	97	44.33%	48.50%
SPX	Adv > Dec 3 days in a row	Below 200-day MA	1 week	-0.65%	-0.04%	44	97	45.36%	48.30%
SPX	Adv < Dec 1 day in a row	Below 200-day MA	1 day	0.06%	0.00%	179	352	50.85%	48.60%
SPX	Adv < Dec 1 day in a row	Below 200-day MA	2 days	0.22%	-0.01%	188	352	53.41%	48.50%
SPX	Adv < Dec 1 day in a row	Below 200-day MA	1 week	0.22%	-0.04%	183	352	51.99%	48.30%
SPX	Adv < Dec 2 days in a row	Below 200-day MA	1 day	0.28%	0.00%	108	190	56.84%	48.60%
SPX	Adv < Dec 2 days in a row	Below 200-day MA	2 days	0.37%	-0.01%	103	190	54.21%	48.50%
SPX	Adv < Dec 2 days in a row	Below 200-day MA	1 week	0.40%	-0.04%	102	190	53.68%	48.30%
SPX	Adv < Dec 3 days in a row	Below 200-day MA	1 day	0.16%	0.00%	53	101	52.48%	48.60%
SPX	Adv < Dec 3 days in a row	Below 200-day MA	2 days	0.20%	-0.01%	54	101	53.47%	48.50%
SPX	Adv < Dec 3 days in a row	Below 200-day MA	1 week	0.47%	-0.04%	54	101	53.47%	48.30%

See page 17 for column descriptions.

Index	Rule 1	Rule 2	Time Period	Gain/Loss	Benchmark Avg	# Winners	# Days	% Profitable	% Profitable Benchmark
NDX	Adv > 2*Dec for one day		1 day	0.30%	0.07%	59	112	52.68%	53.40%
NDX	Adv > 2*Dec for one day		2 days	0.21%	0.14%	63	112	56.25%	52.40%
NDX	Adv > 2*Dec for one day		1 week	-0.05%	0.34%	63	111	56.76%	54.80%
NDX	Adv > 3*Dec for one day		1 day	0.12%	0.07%	11	22	50.00%	53.40%
NDX	Adv > 3*Dec for one day		2 days	0.39%	0.14%	11	22	50.00%	52.40%
NDX	Adv > 3*Dec for one day		1 week	-0.25%	0.34%	12	22	54.55%	54.80%
NDX	Adv*2 < Dec for one day		1 day	0.08%	0.07%	103	199	51.76%	53.40%
NDX	Adv*2 < Dec for one day		2 days	0.14%	0.14%	102	199	51.26%	52.40%
NDX	Adv*2 < Dec for one day		1 week	0.56%	0.34%	106	199	53.27%	54.80%
NDX	Adv*3 < Dec for one day		1 day	0.29%	0.07%	23	45	51.11%	53.40%
NDX	Adv*3 < Dec for one day		2 days	0.59%	0.14%	26	45	57.78%	52.40%
NDX	Adv*3 < Dec for one day		1 week	1.19%	0.34%	26	45	57.78%	54.80%
NDX	Adv > Dec 1 day in a row		1 day	0.03%	0.07%	473	887	53.33%	53.40%
NDX	Adv > Dec 1 day in a row		2 days	-0.04%	0.14%	457	887	51.52%	52.40%
NDX	Adv > Dec 1 day in a row		1 week	0.04%	0.34%	481	885	54.35%	54.80%
NDX	Adv > Dec 2 days in a row		1 day	-0.08%	0.07%	248	486	51.03%	53.40%
NDX	Adv > Dec 2 days in a row		2 days	-0.12%	0.14%	257	486	52.88%	52.40%
NDX	Adv > Dec 2 days in a row		1 week	-0.23%	0.34%	259	485	53.40%	54.80%
NDX	Adv > Dec 3 days in a row		1 day	-0.03%	0.07%	139	264	52.65%	53.40%
NDX	Adv > Dec 3 days in a row		2 days	-0.19%	0.14%	149	263	56.65%	52.40%
NDX	Adv > Dec 3 days in a row		1 week	-0.23%	0.34%	142	263	53.99%	54.80%
NDX	Adv < Dec 1 day in a row		1 day	0.12%	0.07%	514	962	53.43%	53.40%
NDX	Adv < Dec 1 day in a row		2 days	0.31%	0.14%	511	963	53.06%	52.40%
NDX	Adv < Dec 1 day in a row		1 week	0.62%	0.34%	531	962	55.20%	54.80%
NDX	Adv < Dec 2 days in a row		1 day	0.23%	0.07%	307	563	54.53%	53.40%
NDX	Adv < Dec 2 days in a row		2 days	0.40%	0.14%	299	563	53.11%	52.40%
NDX	Adv < Dec 2 days in a row		1 week	0.81%	0.34%	316	563	56.13%	54.80%
NDX	Adv < Dec 3 days in a row		1 day	0.29%	0.07%	182	333	54.65%	53.40%
NDX	Adv < Dec 3 days in a row		2 days	0.42%	0.14%	174	334	52.10%	52.40%
NDX	Adv < Dec 3 days in a row		1 week	0.88%	0.34%	185	334	55.39%	54.80%
NDX	Adv > Dec 1 day in a row	Above 200-day MA	1 day	0.08%	0.12%	342	617	55.43%	55.70%
NDX	Adv > Dec 1 day in a row	Above 200-day MA	2 days	0.16%	0.27%	336	617	54.46%	55.10%
NDX	Adv > Dec 1 day in a row	Above 200-day MA	1 week	0.45%	0.68%	365	615	59.35%	59.60%
NDX	Adv > Dec 2 days in a row	Above 200-day MA	1 day	-0.02%	0.12%	187	358	52.23%	55.70%
NDX	Adv > Dec 2 days in a row	Above 200-day MA	2 days	0.06%	0.27%	199	358	55.59%	55.10%
NDX	Adv > Dec 2 days in a row	Above 200-day MA	1 week	0.09%	0.68%	207	357	57.98%	59.60%
NDX	Adv > Dec 3 days in a row	Above 200-day MA	1 day	0.05%	0.12%	113	203	55.67%	55.70%
NDX	Adv > Dec 3 days in a row	Above 200-day MA	2 days	0.08%	0.27%	122	202	60.40%	55.10%
NDX	Adv > Dec 3 days in a row	Above 200-day MA	1 week	0.14%	0.68%	117	202	57.92%	59.60%
NDX	Adv < Dec 1 day in a row	Above 200-day MA	1 day	0.17%	0.12%	329	589	55.86%	55.70%
NDX	Adv < Dec 1 day in a row	Above 200-day MA	2 days	0.38%	0.27%	328	589	55.69%	55.10%
NDX	Adv < Dec 1 day in a row	Above 200-day MA	1 week	0.91%	0.68%	351	588	59.69%	59.60%
NDX	Adv < Dec 2 days in a row	Above 200-day MA	1 day	0.20%	0.12%	188	329	57.14%	55.70%
NDX	Adv < Dec 2 days in a row	Above 200-day MA	2 days	0.41%	0.27%	184	329	55.93%	55.10%
NDX	Adv < Dec 2 days in a row	Above 200-day MA	1 week	0.88%	0.68%	196	329	59.57%	59.60%
NDX	Adv < Dec 3 days in a row	Above 200-day MA	1 day	0.23%	0.12%	104	182	57.14%	55.70%
NDX	Adv < Dec 3 days in a row	Above 200-day MA	2 days	0.43%	0.27%	100	182	54.95%	55.10%
NDX	Adv < Dec 3 days in a row	Above 200-day MA	1 week	0.86%	0.68%	110	182	60.44%	59.60%
NDX	Adv > Dec 1 day in a row	Below 200-day MA	1 day	-0.08%	-0.02%	131	270	48.52%	49.10%
NDX	Adv > Dec 1 day in a row	Below 200-day MA	2 days	-0.48%	-0.09%	121	270	44.81%	47.20%
NDX	Adv > Dec 1 day in a row	Below 200-day MA	1 week	-0.90%	-0.29%	116	270	42.96%	46.00%
NDX	Adv > Dec 2 days in a row	Below 200-day MA	1 day	-0.24%	-0.02%	61	128	47.66%	49.10%
NDX	Adv > Dec 2 days in a row	Below 200-day MA	2 days	-0.61%	-0.09%	58	128	45.31%	47.20%
NDX	Adv > Dec 2 days in a row	Below 200-day MA	1 week	-1.14%	-0.29%	52	128	40.63%	46.00%
NDX	Adv > Dec 3 days in a row	Below 200-day MA	1 day	-0.30%	-0.02%	26	61	42.62%	49.10%
NDX	Adv > Dec 3 days in a row	Below 200-day MA	2 days	-1.09%	-0.09%	27	61	44.26%	47.20%
NDX	Adv > Dec 3 days in a row	Below 200-day MA	1 week	-1.45%	-0.29%	25	61	40.98%	46.00%
NDX	Adv < Dec 1 day in a row	Below 200-day MA	1 day	0.03%	-0.02%	185	373	49.60%	49.10%
NDX	Adv < Dec 1 day in a row	Below 200-day MA	2 days	0.19%	-0.09%	183	374	48.93%	47.20%
NDX	Adv < Dec 1 day in a row	Below 200-day MA	1 week	0.16%	-0.29%	180	374	48.13%	46.00%
NDX	Adv < Dec 2 days in a row	Below 200-day MA	1 day	0.27%	-0.02%	119	233	51.07%	49.10%
NDX	Adv < Dec 2 days in a row	Below 200-day MA	2 days	0.40%	-0.09%	115	234	49.15%	47.20%
NDX	Adv < Dec 2 days in a row	Below 200-day MA	1 week	0.73%	-0.29%	120	234	51.28%	46.00%
NDX	Adv < Dec 3 days in a row	Below 200-day MA	1 day	0.36%	-0.02%	78	151	51.66%	49.10%
NDX	Adv < Dec 3 days in a row	Below 200-day MA	2 days	0.40%	-0.09%	74	152	48.68%	47.20%
NDX	Adv < Dec 3 days in a row	Below 200-day MA	1 week	0.90%	-0.29%	75	152	49.34%	46.00%

SUMMARY AND CONCLUSION

These results are at odds with the way the majority of Wall Street interprets advancing and declining issues and is at odds with the way the financial markets press reports the news. Whether or not these findings will hold in the future is hard to say, but they philosophically and statistically fall in line with many of the other tests published here.

In conclusion, these results show that it has been better to be selectively buying the SPX and the NDX when market breadth has been poor versus when market breadth has been strong.

We'll now move to looking at market volume and its relationship to price movement.

CHAPTER **6**

VOLUME

■ ■

We are aware of many books and articles written on the role that volume plays in predicting short-term movement in stock prices, but we are not aware of many statistical studies to back these claims. This is surprising considering how popular volume is as an indicator and just how much it is relied upon by traders and investors. In this chapter, we'll look at a combination of volume and price in order to see if there is an edge.

In many sections in this book, we found evidence that the setup or indicator used has led to an edge in the markets over the past one to two decades. Interestingly, in looking at volume, which is an indicator that is most often quoted by the media and many professionals, the results were mixed. We know these findings will be of most interest because many traders use volume to interpret and identify trading situations. Based upon the test data presented below, we were surprised to find these inconsistent results and outside of one scenario (see number 5 below), there was no discernable edge (we did not look at low volume days as many of those days coincide with holidays, shortened trading sessions, etc.).

A summary of our findings is as follows:

Large Volume Days Alone Are Insignificant

1. If you look at the average daily gain of the SPX and the NDX on the day that has the highest volume in a week, you'll see very mixed re-

sults. The 1-day SPX return was better than the average daily return but the 1-day NDX return was well under the average. The 1-week SPX return was near the average return and the monthly return outperformed. Both the weekly and NDX returns came in under the overall average. Mixed results here and certainly no clear evidence of any edge looking only at days with big volume.

2. We then looked at the market when it had a large x day volume move and also when the market rose for the day. As you will see, the results were again mixed and led to no obvious conclusions.

3. We looked at the same parameters as #2 except we looked at those days where the market dropped for the day. Again, there was no definitive edge as the returns were inconsistent.

4. In other studies published in this book, when we added a trend component (the 200-day moving average) to the indicator, it often made the results of that indicator better. This was not the case with volume. Once again, the results were inconclusive.

Large Up Days Accompanied by Large Volume Were Significant

5. There was one place where we did find an edge and it's a healthy one: When prices had their biggest up day over the past 10 days and their biggest volume day the same day, the returns over the next day were on average up .25%. For the next week they were up .60% and for the next month they were 1.45%. These results tell us that a short-term edge seems to exist when you isolate a large up move that coincides with healthy volume. This is consistent with the concepts taught by William O'Neil and *Investor's Business Daily*.

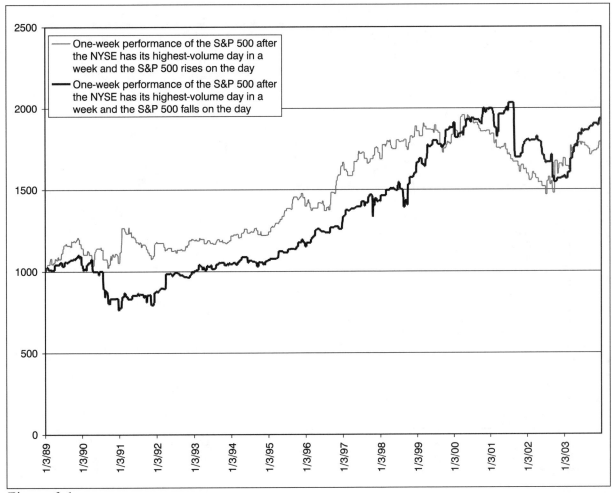

Figure 6-1

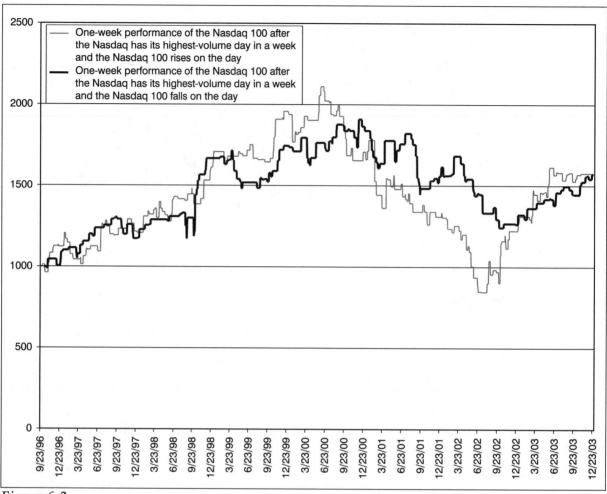

Figure 6-2

Index	Rule 1	Rule 2	Time Period	Gain/Loss	Benchmark Avg	# Winners	# Days	% Profitable	% Profitable Benchmark
SPX	Most volume in 1 week		1 day	0.08%	0.04%	442	833	53.06%	52.71%
SPX	Most volume in 1 week		2 days	0.06%	0.08%	441	833	52.94%	54.11%
SPX	Most volume in 1 week		1 week	0.21%	0.21%	466	834	55.88%	56.66%
SPX	Most volume in 1 month		1 day	0.00%	0.04%	101	220	45.91%	52.71%
SPX	Most volume in 1 month		2 days	-0.07%	0.08%	111	220	50.45%	54.11%
SPX	Most volume in 1 month		1 week	0.27%	0.21%	123	220	55.91%	56.66%
SPX	Most volume in 1 week	Market rises today	1 day	0.05%	0.04%	235	459	51.20%	52.71%
SPX	Most volume in 1 week	Market rises today	2 days	0.09%	0.08%	245	459	53.38%	54.11%
SPX	Most volume in 1 week	Market rises today	1 week	0.17%	0.21%	258	460	56.09%	56.66%
SPX	Most volume in 1 month	Market rises today	1 day	0.04%	0.04%	53	117	45.30%	52.71%
SPX	Most volume in 1 month	Market rises today	2 days	0.11%	0.08%	64	117	54.70%	54.11%
SPX	Most volume in 1 month	Market rises today	1 week	0.57%	0.21%	68	117	58.12%	56.66%
SPX	Most volume in 1 week	Market falls today	1 day	0.11%	0.04%	207	373	55.50%	52.71%
SPX	Most volume in 1 week	Market falls today	2 days	0.03%	0.08%	196	373	52.55%	54.11%
SPX	Most volume in 1 week	Market falls today	1 week	0.25%	0.21%	207	373	55.50%	56.66%
SPX	Most volume in 1 month	Market falls today	1 day	-0.06%	0.04%	48	102	47.06%	52.71%
SPX	Most volume in 1 month	Market falls today	2 days	-0.28%	0.08%	47	102	46.08%	54.11%
SPX	Most volume in 1 month	Market falls today	1 week	-0.08%	0.21%	54	102	52.94%	56.66%
SPX	Most vol in 1 wk, market rises today	Above 200-day MA	1 day	0.06%	0.05%	185	356	51.97%	53.49%
SPX	Most vol in 1 wk, market rises today	Above 200-day MA	2 days	0.09%	0.10%	192	356	53.93%	55.56%
SPX	Most vol in 1 wk, market rises today	Above 200-day MA	1 week	0.16%	0.25%	200	357	56.02%	58.22%
SPX	Most vol in 1 mth, market rises today	Above 200-day MA	1 day	-0.02%	0.05%	41	95	43.16%	53.49%
SPX	Most vol in 1 mth, market rises today	Above 200-day MA	2 days	0.04%	0.10%	50	95	52.63%	55.56%
SPX	Most vol in 1 mth, market rises today	Above 200-day MA	1 week	0.38%	0.25%	55	95	57.89%	58.22%
SPX	Most vol in 1 wk, market falls today	Above 200-day MA	1 day	0.00%	0.05%	130	245	53.06%	53.49%
SPX	Most vol in 1 wk, market falls today	Above 200-day MA	2 days	-0.08%	0.10%	122	245	49.80%	55.56%
SPX	Most vol in 1 wk, market falls today	Above 200-day MA	1 week	0.30%	0.25%	138	245	56.33%	58.22%
SPX	Most vol in 1 mth, market falls today	Above 200-day MA	1 day	-0.10%	0.05%	26	55	47.27%	53.49%
SPX	Most vol in 1 mth, market falls today	Above 200-day MA	2 days	-0.17%	0.10%	25	55	45.45%	55.56%
SPX	Most vol in 1 mth, market falls today	Above 200-day MA	1 week	0.48%	0.25%	34	55	61.82%	58.22%
SPX	Most vol in 1 wk, market rises today	Below 200-day MA	1 day	0.02%	0.02%	50	103	48.54%	50.63%
SPX	Most vol in 1 wk, market rises today	Below 200-day MA	2 days	0.07%	0.04%	53	103	51.46%	50.24%
SPX	Most vol in 1 wk, market rises today	Below 200-day MA	1 week	0.20%	0.09%	58	103	56.31%	52.48%
SPX	Most vol in 1 mth, market rises today	Below 200-day MA	1 day	0.31%	0.02%	12	22	54.55%	50.63%
SPX	Most vol in 1 mth, market rises today	Below 200-day MA	2 days	0.40%	0.04%	14	22	63.64%	50.24%
SPX	Most vol in 1 mth, market rises today	Below 200-day MA	1 week	1.40%	0.09%	13	22	59.09%	52.48%
SPX	Most vol in 1 wk, market falls today	Below 200-day MA	1 day	0.32%	0.02%	77	128	60.16%	50.63%
SPX	Most vol in 1 wk, market falls today	Below 200-day MA	2 days	0.23%	0.04%	74	128	57.81%	50.24%
SPX	Most vol in 1 wk, market falls today	Below 200-day MA	1 week	0.16%	0.09%	69	128	53.91%	52.48%
SPX	Most vol in 1 mth, market falls today	Below 200-day MA	1 day	-0.01%	0.02%	22	47	46.81%	50.63%
SPX	Most vol in 1 mth, market falls today	Below 200-day MA	2 days	-0.40%	0.04%	22	47	46.81%	50.24%
SPX	Most vol in 1 mth, market falls today	Below 200-day MA	1 week	-0.74%	0.09%	20	47	42.55%	52.48%

See page 17 for column descriptions.

ndex	Rule 1	Rule 2	Time Period	Gain/Loss	Benchmark Avg	# Winners	# Days	% Profitable	% Profitable Benchmark
NDX	Most volume in 1 week		1 day	0.12%	0.07%	218	400	54.50%	53.33%
NDX	Most volume in 1 week		2 days	0.11%	0.14%	197	399	49.37%	52.21%
NDX	Most volume in 1 week		1 week	0.27%	0.32%	209	398	52.51%	54.70%
NDX	Most volume in 1 month		1 day	-0.12%	0.07%	62	120	51.67%	53.33%
NDX	Most volume in 1 month		2 days	0.03%	0.14%	62	120	51.67%	52.21%
NDX	Most volume in 1 month		1 week	0.61%	0.32%	69	120	57.50%	54.70%
NDX	Most volume in 1 week	Market rises today	1 day	0.01%	0.07%	119	225	52.89%	53.33%
NDX	Most volume in 1 week	Market rises today	2 days	-0.12%	0.14%	108	225	48.00%	52.21%
NDX	Most volume in 1 week	Market rises today	1 week	0.26%	0.32%	119	224	53.13%	54.70%
NDX	Most volume in 1 month	Market rises today	1 day	-0.40%	0.07%	31	67	46.27%	53.33%
NDX	Most volume in 1 month	Market rises today	2 days	-0.51%	0.14%	30	67	44.78%	52.21%
NDX	Most volume in 1 month	Market rises today	1 week	0.75%	0.32%	42	67	62.69%	54.70%
NDX	Most volume in 1 week	Market falls today	1 day	0.31%	0.07%	99	173	57.23%	53.33%
NDX	Most volume in 1 week	Market falls today	2 days	0.44%	0.14%	89	172	51.74%	52.21%
NDX	Most volume in 1 week	Market falls today	1 week	0.33%	0.32%	90	172	52.33%	54.70%
NDX	Most volume in 1 month	Market falls today	1 day	0.32%	0.07%	31	52	59.62%	53.33%
NDX	Most volume in 1 month	Market falls today	2 days	0.81%	0.14%	32	52	61.54%	52.21%
NDX	Most volume in 1 month	Market falls today	1 week	0.55%	0.32%	27	52	51.92%	54.70%
NDX	Most vol in 1 wk, market rises today	Above 200-day MA	1 day	0.03%	0.12%	79	148	53.38%	55.59%
NDX	Most vol in 1 wk, market rises today	Above 200-day MA	2 days	0.01%	0.26%	76	148	51.35%	54.92%
NDX	Most vol in 1 wk, market rises today	Above 200-day MA	1 week	0.61%	0.65%	86	147	58.50%	59.44%
NDX	Most vol in 1 mth, market rises today	Above 200-day MA	1 day	-0.18%	0.12%	23	45	51.11%	55.59%
NDX	Most vol in 1 mth, market rises today	Above 200-day MA	2 days	-0.38%	0.26%	21	45	46.67%	54.92%
NDX	Most vol in 1 mth, market rises today	Above 200-day MA	1 week	0.76%	0.65%	30	45	66.67%	59.44%
NDX	Most vol in 1 wk, market falls today	Above 200-day MA	1 day	0.24%	0.12%	62	105	59.05%	55.59%
NDX	Most vol in 1 wk, market falls today	Above 200-day MA	2 days	0.26%	0.26%	57	104	54.81%	54.92%
NDX	Most vol in 1 wk, market falls today	Above 200-day MA	1 week	0.38%	0.65%	56	104	53.85%	59.44%
NDX	Most vol in 1 mth, market falls today	Above 200-day MA	1 day	0.36%	0.12%	24	35	68.57%	55.59%
NDX	Most vol in 1 mth, market falls today	Above 200-day MA	2 days	0.41%	0.26%	23	35	65.71%	54.92%
NDX	Most vol in 1 mth, market falls today	Above 200-day MA	1 week	0.26%	0.65%	19	35	54.29%	59.44%
NDX	Most vol in 1 wk, market rises today	Below 200-day MA	1 day	-0.02%	-0.02%	40	77	51.95%	49.14%
NDX	Most vol in 1 wk, market rises today	Below 200-day MA	2 days	-0.36%	-0.09%	32	77	41.56%	47.20%
NDX	Most vol in 1 wk, market rises today	Below 200-day MA	1 week	-0.41%	-0.29%	33	77	42.86%	45.96%
NDX	Most vol in 1 mth, market rises today	Below 200-day MA	1 day	-0.84%	-0.02%	8	22	36.36%	49.14%
NDX	Most vol in 1 mth, market rises today	Below 200-day MA	2 days	-0.78%	-0.09%	9	22	40.91%	47.20%
NDX	Most vol in 1 mth, market rises today	Below 200-day MA	1 week	0.74%	-0.29%	12	22	54.55%	45.96%
NDX	Most vol in 1 wk, market falls today	Below 200-day MA	1 day	0.41%	-0.02%	37	68	54.41%	49.14%
NDX	Most vol in 1 wk, market falls today	Below 200-day MA	2 days	0.72%	-0.09%	32	68	47.06%	47.20%
NDX	Most vol in 1 wk, market falls today	Below 200-day MA	1 week	0.26%	-0.29%	34	68	50.00%	45.96%
NDX	Most vol in 1 mth, market falls today	Below 200-day MA	1 day	0.24%	-0.02%	7	17	41.18%	49.14%
NDX	Most vol in 1 mth, market falls today	Below 200-day MA	2 days	1.64%	-0.09%	9	17	52.94%	47.20%
NDX	Most vol in 1 mth, market falls today	Below 200-day MA	1 week	1.15%	-0.29%	8	17	47.06%	45.96%

SUMMARY AND CONCLUSION

Is volume important? Perhaps, but the overall results are inconclusive.

In other chapters we used indicators or setups in a stand-alone fashion (as we did in this chapter) and in many of these cases an obvious edge existed. But, in looking at volume as a stand-alone indicator, we could not find an obvious edge outside of the days that had their biggest up day of the past 10 days coinciding with the biggest volume day of the past 10 days.

We are not saying that volume does not have an impact in helping predict future price direction. Obviously, our testing was limited to the most obvious ways to apply volume. Based upon the tests we ran, the edge is strongest when you combine both price and volume. Large volume by itself is not significant.

CHAPTER **7**

LARGE MOVES

■ ■

Large one-day moves create a great deal of excitement. When prices rise sharply, you can feel the burst of energy it creates as analysts and financial market journalists excitedly tell us the good news as to why prices rose. And, they usually go further by saying that today's big move up is likely to lead to a further rise in prices.

When prices drop significantly, the opposite is true. Bad economic news, poor earnings and negative outlooks all become part of the nightly equation as to why prices dropped. And, this negative psychology many times tends to then manifest itself in justifying why the outlook for the stock market is poor.

We looked at large moves in the SPX and the NDX over a 15-year period (January 1, 1989–December 31, 2003). For both markets, we looked at the days that rose or fell more than 1% and more than 2% (one should note, especially when looking at the time graphs, that the number of large daily moves increased in the late 1990s as volatility increased).

A sample of our findings is as follows:

Large Price Declines Outperform Large Price Gains

1. The most significant finding was that large declines in the SPX outperformed the average day by a better than 2-1 margin after 2 days and

after a week when the drop was 1% or more. When the drop was 2% or more, the performance jumped even more significantly.

Large Positive Moves in the SPX Have Been Followed by Further Gains

2. The SPX rising 1% or more and 2% or more also led to outperformance. This was not true for the NDX.

Large Declines in the Nasdaq 100 Have Been Positive

3. Large declines in the NDX outperformed large rises.

Declines Above the 200-Day Moving Average Were Significant

4. Two-percent drops for both the SPX when above the 200-day moving average have led to significant large outperformance versus the benchmark. It also outperformed in the NDX for 2 days and a week.

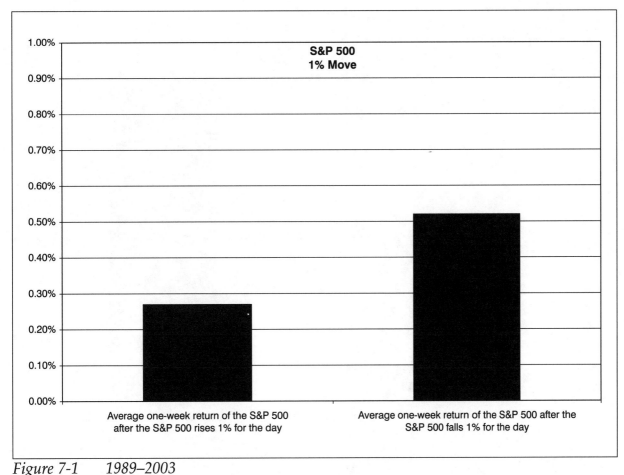

Figure 7-1   1989–2003

1% Declines Have Outperformed 1% Gains in the S&P 500 After 1 Week

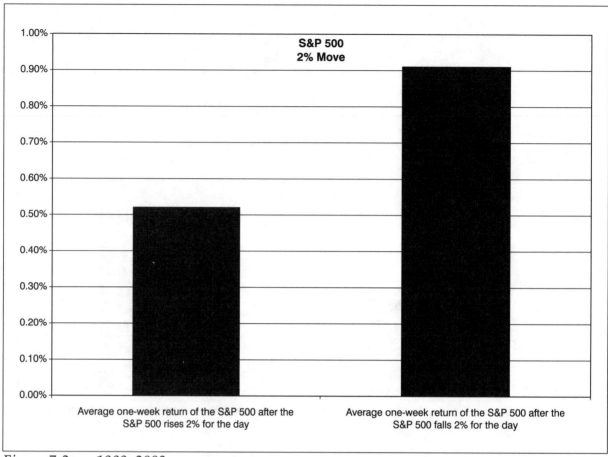

Figure 7-2   1989–2003

2% Declines Have Outperformed 2% Gains in the S&P 500 After 1 Week

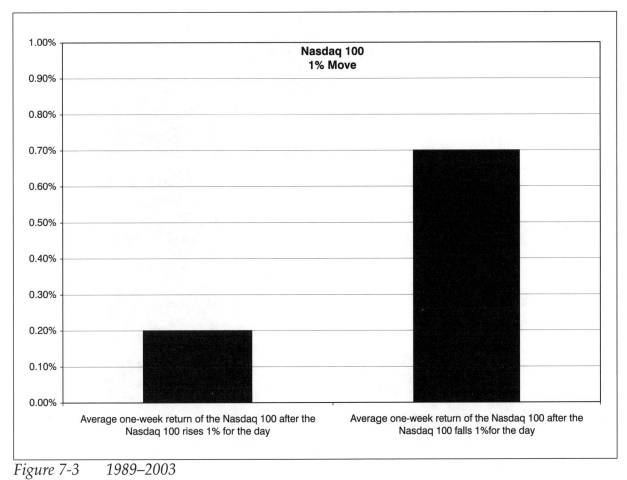

Figure 7-3   1989–2003

1% Nasdaq Losses Have Outperformed 1% Nasdaq Gains by a 3-1 Margin Over 1 Week

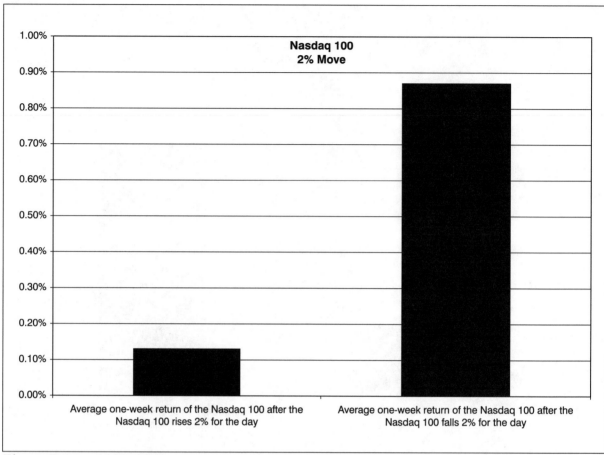

Figure 7-4   1989–2003

2% Nasdaq Losses Have Outperformed 2% Nasdaq Gains by a Better Than 5-1 Margin After 1 Week

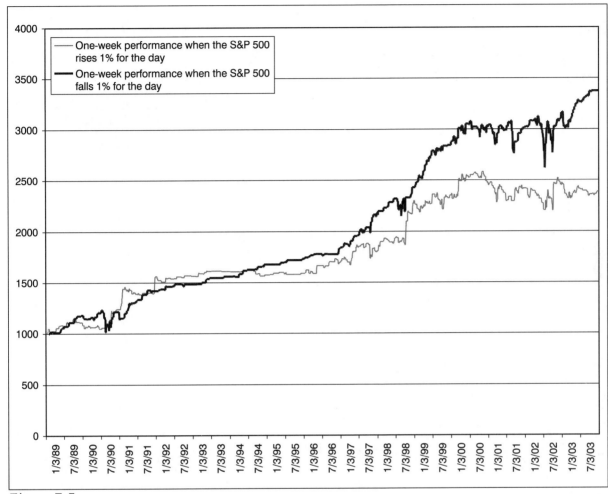

Figure 7-5

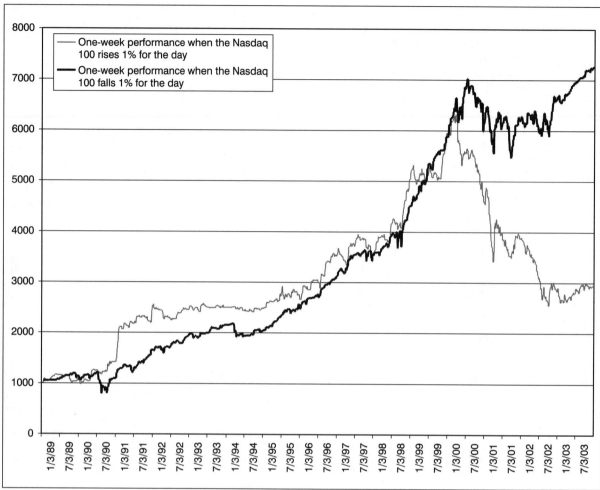

Figure 7-6

Index	Rule 1	Rule 2	Time Period	Gain/Loss	Benchmark Avg	# Winners	# Days	% Profitable	% Profitable Benchmark
SPX	Rises 1%		1 day	0.13%	0.04%	260	508	51.18%	52.71%
SPX	Rises 1%		2 days	0.14%	0.08%	275	508	54.13%	54.11%
SPX	Rises 1%		1 week	0.27%	0.21%	276	507	54.44%	56.66%
SPX	Rises 2%		1 day	0.16%	0.04%	61	112	54.46%	52.71%
SPX	Rises 2%		2 days	0.20%	0.08%	62	112	55.36%	54.11%
SPX	Rises 2%		1 week	0.52%	0.21%	68	112	60.71%	56.66%
SPX	Falls 1%		1 day	0.07%	0.04%	249	456	54.61%	52.71%
SPX	Falls 1%		2 days	0.19%	0.08%	255	456	55.92%	54.11%
SPX	Falls 1%		1 week	0.52%	0.21%	262	456	57.46%	56.66%
SPX	Falls 2%		1 day	0.28%	0.04%	68	110	61.82%	52.71%
SPX	Falls 2%		2 days	0.47%	0.08%	67	110	60.91%	54.11%
SPX	Falls 2%		1 week	0.91%	0.21%	66	110	60.00%	56.66%
SPX	Rises 1%	Above 200-day MA	1 day	0.09%	0.05%	171	332	51.51%	53.49%
SPX	Rises 1%	Above 200-day MA	2 days	0.15%	0.10%	187	332	56.33%	55.56%
SPX	Rises 1%	Above 200-day MA	1 week	0.25%	0.25%	182	331	54.98%	58.22%
SPX	Rises 2%	Above 200-day MA	1 day	0.13%	0.05%	28	52	53.85%	53.49%
SPX	Rises 2%	Above 200-day MA	2 days	0.13%	0.10%	30	52	57.69%	55.56%
SPX	Rises 2%	Above 200-day MA	1 week	0.50%	0.25%	34	52	65.38%	58.22%
SPX	Falls 1%	Above 200-day MA	1 day	0.13%	0.05%	125	214	58.41%	53.49%
SPX	Falls 1%	Above 200-day MA	2 days	0.19%	0.10%	122	214	57.01%	55.56%
SPX	Falls 1%	Above 200-day MA	1 week	0.72%	0.25%	134	214	62.62%	58.22%
SPX	Falls 2%	Above 200-day MA	1 day	0.56%	0.05%	26	35	74.29%	53.49%
SPX	Falls 2%	Above 200-day MA	2 days	0.60%	0.10%	23	35	65.71%	55.56%
SPX	Falls 2%	Above 200-day MA	1 week	0.97%	0.25%	20	35	57.14%	58.22%
SPX	Rises 1%	Below 200-day MA	1 day	0.18%	0.02%	89	176	50.57%	50.63%
SPX	Rises 1%	Below 200-day MA	2 days	0.13%	0.04%	88	176	50.00%	50.24%
SPX	Rises 1%	Below 200-day MA	1 week	0.31%	0.09%	94	176	53.41%	52.48%
SPX	Rises 2%	Below 200-day MA	1 day	0.19%	0.02%	33	60	55.00%	50.63%
SPX	Rises 2%	Below 200-day MA	2 days	0.27%	0.04%	32	60	53.33%	50.24%
SPX	Rises 2%	Below 200-day MA	1 week	0.54%	0.09%	34	60	56.67%	52.48%
SPX	Falls 1%	Below 200-day MA	1 day	0.02%	0.02%	124	242	51.24%	50.63%
SPX	Falls 1%	Below 200-day MA	2 days	0.18%	0.04%	133	242	54.96%	50.24%
SPX	Falls 1%	Below 200-day MA	1 week	0.35%	0.09%	128	242	52.89%	52.48%
SPX	Falls 2%	Below 200-day MA	1 day	0.15%	0.02%	42	75	56.00%	50.63%
SPX	Falls 2%	Below 200-day MA	2 days	0.41%	0.04%	44	75	58.67%	50.24%
SPX	Falls 2%	Below 200-day MA	1 week	0.88%	0.09%	46	75	61.33%	52.48%

See page 17 for column descriptions.

ndex	Rule 1	Rule 2	Time Period	Gain/Loss	Benchmark Avg	# Winners	# Days	% Profitable	% Profitable Benchmark
NDX	Rises 1%		1 day	0.09%	0.08%	542	991	54.69%	54.14%
NDX	Rises 1%		2 days	0.06%	0.15%	529	992	53.33%	53.46%
NDX	Rises 1%		1 week	0.20%	0.37%	555	991	56.00%	56.36%
NDX	Rises 2%		1 day	0.01%	0.08%	234	443	52.82%	54.14%
NDX	Rises 2%		2 days	-0.11%	0.15%	231	444	52.03%	53.46%
NDX	Rises 2%		1 week	0.13%	0.37%	242	444	54.50%	56.36%
NDX	Falls 1%		1 day	0.06%	0.08%	468	889	52.64%	54.14%
NDX	Falls 1%		2 days	0.32%	0.15%	486	891	54.55%	53.46%
NDX	Falls 1%		1 week	0.70%	0.37%	510	891	57.24%	56.36%
NDX	Falls 2%		1 day	0.19%	0.08%	235	428	54.91%	54.14%
NDX	Falls 2%		2 days	0.48%	0.15%	242	428	56.54%	53.46%
NDX	Falls 2%		1 week	0.87%	0.37%	246	428	57.48%	56.36%
NDX	Rises 1%	Above 200-day MA	1 day	0.10%	0.09%	394	717	54.95%	54.96%
NDX	Rises 1%	Above 200-day MA	2 days	0.17%	0.19%	395	718	55.01%	54.80%
NDX	Rises 1%	Above 200-day MA	1 week	0.45%	0.49%	425	717	59.27%	58.40%
NDX	Rises 2%	Above 200-day MA	1 day	0.01%	0.09%	149	283	52.65%	54.96%
NDX	Rises 2%	Above 200-day MA	2 days	0.09%	0.19%	154	284	54.23%	54.80%
NDX	Rises 2%	Above 200-day MA	1 week	0.53%	0.49%	167	284	58.80%	58.40%
NDX	Falls 1%	Above 200-day MA	1 day	0.07%	0.09%	287	530	54.15%	54.96%
NDX	Falls 1%	Above 200-day MA	2 days	0.29%	0.19%	300	530	56.60%	54.80%
NDX	Falls 1%	Above 200-day MA	1 week	0.75%	0.49%	311	530	58.68%	58.40%
NDX	Falls 2%	Above 200-day MA	1 day	0.29%	0.09%	119	201	59.20%	54.96%
NDX	Falls 2%	Above 200-day MA	2 days	0.47%	0.19%	121	201	60.20%	54.80%
NDX	Falls 2%	Above 200-day MA	1 week	1.07%	0.49%	121	201	60.20%	58.40%
NDX	Rises 1%	Below 200-day MA	1 day	0.06%	0.03%	148	274	54.01%	52.03%
NDX	Rises 1%	Below 200-day MA	2 days	-0.23%	0.04%	134	274	48.91%	49.91%
NDX	Rises 1%	Below 200-day MA	1 week	-0.48%	0.06%	130	274	47.45%	51.13%
NDX	Rises 2%	Below 200-day MA	1 day	0.03%	0.03%	85	160	53.13%	52.03%
NDX	Rises 2%	Below 200-day MA	2 days	-0.46%	0.04%	77	160	48.13%	49.91%
NDX	Rises 2%	Below 200-day MA	1 week	-0.57%	0.06%	75	160	46.88%	51.13%
NDX	Falls 1%	Below 200-day MA	1 day	0.05%	0.03%	181	359	50.42%	52.03%
NDX	Falls 1%	Below 200-day MA	2 days	0.36%	0.04%	186	361	51.52%	49.91%
NDX	Falls 1%	Below 200-day MA	1 week	0.63%	0.06%	199	361	55.12%	51.13%
NDX	Falls 2%	Below 200-day MA	1 day	0.10%	0.03%	116	227	51.10%	52.03%
NDX	Falls 2%	Below 200-day MA	2 days	0.49%	0.04%	121	227	53.30%	49.91%
NDX	Falls 2%	Below 200-day MA	1 week	0.70%	0.06%	125	227	55.07%	51.13%

SUMMARY AND CONCLUSION

It appears that large market drops are followed by immediate snap back moves. This is especially true during the times the S&P 500 has traded above its 200-day moving average. After panic has set in and the selling is finished, the market many times has quickly recovered and these recoveries are often strong.

Now let's see how the market has done when an abundance of stocks were making new 52-week highs or 52-week lows.

CHAPTER **8**

NEW 52-WEEK HIGHS, NEW 52-WEEK LOWS

It is widely assumed that the more stocks making new 52-week highs, the healthier the market is, and this healthy condition is often a prelude to further upward movement. And, it's also widely assumed that the more stocks making new 52-week lows, the weaker the market condition is and the weaker the outlook is for stocks. These assumptions appear to be wrong.

We used the HILO Index for looking at these assumptions. The HILO Index is a daily number that subtracts the number of new 52-week lows for the day from the number of new 52-week highs for the day (new 52-week highs minus new 52-week lows). The higher the number, the more stocks made new highs versus new lows. A negative number means that more stocks made new 52-week lows for the day than 52-week highs.

We looked at the data from January 2, 1990 through December 31, 2003. We looked at the HILO INDEX making a new 1-week high (low), a new 5-week high (low), and a new 10-week high (low). What we found was that 1-week lows, 5-week lows and 10-week lows of the HILO Index outperform 1-, 5- and 10-week highs over a 1-week and 2-week period. We see the same thing for the Nasdaq market. This is further seen in looking at results both above and below the 200-day moving average as the market on a whole has done better after the HILO Index made new short-term lows versus made new short-term highs. These findings are consistent with many of the findings in other chapters that show it's been better to be a buyer on short-term weakness versus being a buyer after market strength has occurred.

Multiple new highs appear to be healthy for the market as seen by the fact that they outperform the benchmark over a short-term period of time. But, even better is when the number of new highs versus new lows is at a low extreme. These times tend to lead to rallies that have on average outperformed the average 1-week and 2-week gains the market has seen over the 14-year period of time tested.

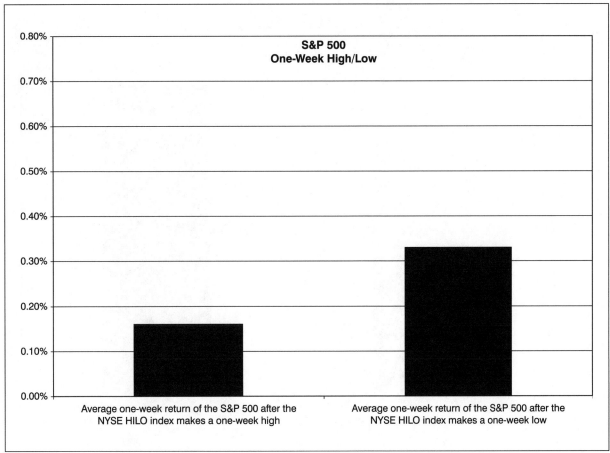

Figure 8-1   1990–2003

1-Week Highs in the HILO Index Have Underperformed
1-Week Lows in the HILO Index.

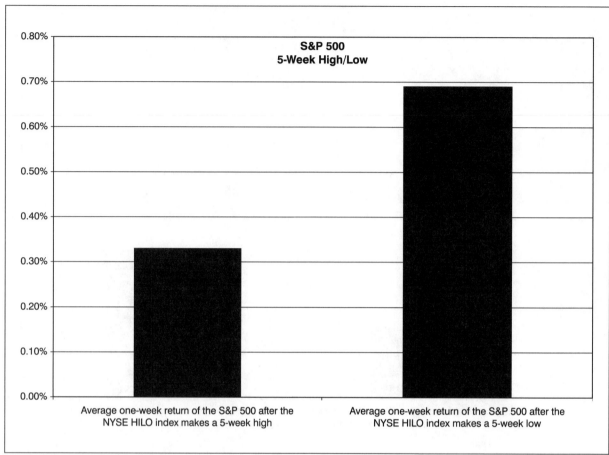

Figure 8-2   1990–2003

5-Week Lows in the HILO Index Have Led to Greater Returns Than 5-Week Highs in the Index

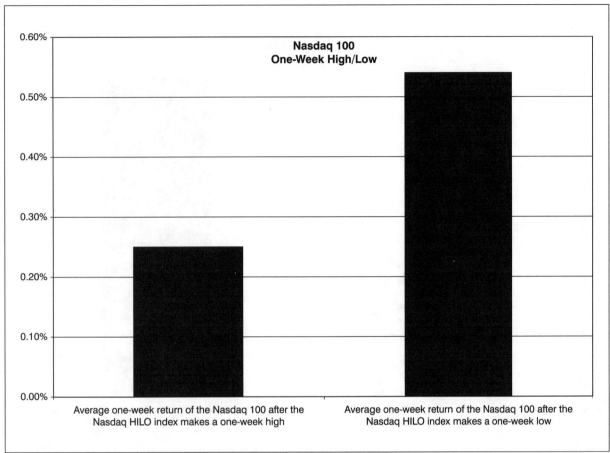

Figure 8-3   1990–2003

The Nasdaq Has Seen Gains of Better Than 2:1 After the HILO Index Made a New 1-Week Low versus a New 1-Week High

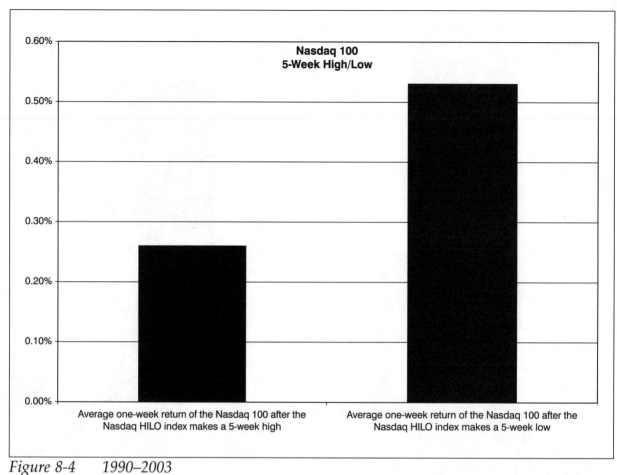

Figure 8-4   1990–2003

*5-Week Lows in the Nasdaq HILO Index Have Outperformed 5-Week Highs
in the Index*

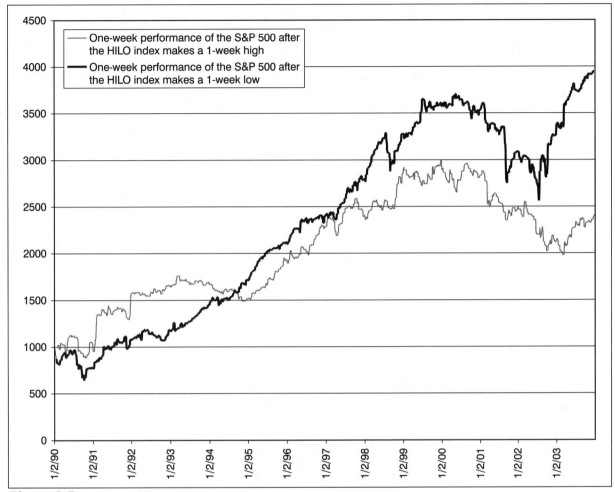

Figure 8-5

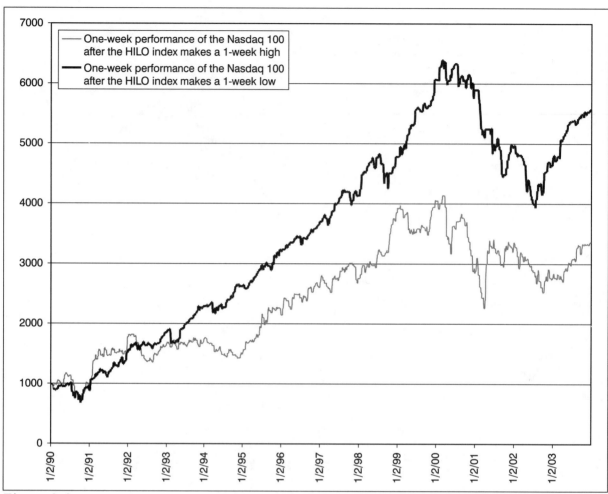

Figure 8-6

Index	Rule 1	Rule 2	Time Period	Gain/Loss	Benchmark Avg	# Winners	# Days	% Profitable	% Profitable Benchmark
SPX	1-wk high of NYSEHILO		1 week	0.16%	0.19%	498	899	55.39%	55.91%
SPX	1-wk high of NYSEHILO		2 weeks	0.27%	0.37%	514	898	57.24%	57.52%
SPX	5-wk high of NYSEHILO		1 week	0.33%	0.19%	158	269	58.74%	55.91%
SPX	5-wk high of NYSEHILO		2 weeks	0.49%	0.37%	162	269	60.22%	57.52%
SPX	10-wk high of NYSEHILO		1 week	0.46%	0.19%	95	155	61.29%	55.91%
SPX	10-wk high of NYSEHILO		2 weeks	0.60%	0.37%	97	155	62.58%	57.52%
SPX	1-wk low of NYSEHILO		1 week	0.33%	0.19%	517	905	57.13%	55.91%
SPX	1-wk low of NYSEHILO		2 weeks	0.56%	0.37%	550	905	60.77%	57.52%
SPX	5-wk low of NYSEHILO		1 week	0.69%	0.19%	155	256	60.55%	55.91%
SPX	5-wk low of NYSEHILO		2 weeks	1.00%	0.37%	169	256	66.02%	57.52%
SPX	10-wk low of NYSEHILO		1 week	0.79%	0.19%	88	150	58.67%	55.91%
SPX	10-wk low of NYSEHILO		2 weeks	1.21%	0.37%	97	150	64.67%	57.52%
SPX	1-wk high of NYSEHILO	Above 200-day MA	1 week	0.21%	0.23%	366	648	56.48%	57.33%
SPX	1-wk high of NYSEHILO	Above 200-day MA	2 weeks	0.47%	0.46%	390	647	60.28%	59.13%
SPX	5-wk high of NYSEHILO	Above 200-day MA	1 week	0.43%	0.23%	121	202	59.90%	57.33%
SPX	5-wk high of NYSEHILO	Above 200-day MA	2 weeks	0.71%	0.46%	130	202	64.36%	59.13%
SPX	10-wk high of NYSEHILO	Above 200-day MA	1 week	0.47%	0.23%	74	123	60.16%	57.33%
SPX	10-wk high of NYSEHILO	Above 200-day MA	2 weeks	0.76%	0.46%	82	123	66.67%	59.13%
SPX	1-wk low of NYSEHILO	Above 200-day MA	1 week	0.34%	0.23%	361	610	59.18%	57.33%
SPX	1-wk low of NYSEHILO	Above 200-day MA	2 weeks	0.49%	0.46%	375	610	61.48%	59.13%
SPX	5-wk low of NYSEHILO	Above 200-day MA	1 week	0.52%	0.23%	98	158	62.03%	57.33%
SPX	5-wk low of NYSEHILO	Above 200-day MA	2 weeks	0.72%	0.46%	104	158	65.82%	59.13%
SPX	10-wk low of NYSEHILO	Above 200-day MA	1 week	0.49%	0.23%	49	85	57.65%	57.33%
SPX	10-wk low of NYSEHILO	Above 200-day MA	2 weeks	0.62%	0.46%	54	85	63.53%	59.13%
SPX	1-wk high of NYSEHILO	Below 200-day MA	1 week	0.03%	0.09%	132	251	52.59%	52.48%
SPX	1-wk high of NYSEHILO	Below 200-day MA	2 weeks	-0.24%	0.17%	124	251	49.40%	53.64%
SPX	5-wk high of NYSEHILO	Below 200-day MA	1 week	0.03%	0.09%	37	67	55.22%	52.48%
SPX	5-wk high of NYSEHILO	Below 200-day MA	2 weeks	-0.19%	0.17%	32	67	47.76%	53.64%
SPX	10-wk high of NYSEHILO	Below 200-day MA	1 week	0.42%	0.09%	21	32	65.63%	52.48%
SPX	10-wk high of NYSEHILO	Below 200-day MA	2 weeks	0.00%	0.17%	15	32	46.88%	53.64%
SPX	1-wk low of NYSEHILO	Below 200-day MA	1 week	0.29%	0.09%	156	295	52.88%	52.48%
SPX	1-wk low of NYSEHILO	Below 200-day MA	2 weeks	0.70%	0.17%	175	295	59.32%	53.64%
SPX	5-wk low of NYSEHILO	Below 200-day MA	1 week	0.96%	0.09%	57	98	58.16%	52.48%
SPX	5-wk low of NYSEHILO	Below 200-day MA	2 weeks	1.45%	0.17%	65	98	66.33%	53.64%
SPX	10-wk low of NYSEHILO	Below 200-day MA	1 week	1.19%	0.09%	39	65	60.00%	52.48%
SPX	10-wk low of NYSEHILO	Below 200-day MA	2 weeks	1.98%	0.17%	43	65	66.15%	53.64%

See page 17 for column descriptions.

Index	Rule 1	Rule 2	Time Period	Gain/Loss	Benchmark Avg	# Winners	# Days	% Profitable	% Profitable Benchmark
NDX	1-wk high of NASDAQHILO		1 week	0.25%	0.36%	518	937	55.28%	55.51%
NDX	1-wk high of NASDAQHILO		2 weeks	0.41%	0.70%	524	936	55.98%	56.43%
NDX	5-wk high of NASDAQHILO		1 week	0.26%	0.36%	158	304	51.97%	55.51%
NDX	5-wk high of NASDAQHILO		2 weeks	0.80%	0.70%	178	304	58.55%	56.43%
NDX	10-wk high of NASDAQHILO		1 week	0.52%	0.36%	96	185	51.89%	55.51%
NDX	10-wk high of NASDAQHILO		2 weeks	1.36%	0.70%	115	185	62.16%	56.43%
NDX	1-wk low of NASDAQHILO		1 week	0.54%	0.36%	487	842	57.84%	55.51%
NDX	1-wk low of NASDAQHILO		2 weeks	0.89%	0.70%	487	841	57.91%	56.43%
NDX	5-wk low of NASDAQHILO		1 week	0.53%	0.36%	147	260	56.54%	55.51%
NDX	5-wk low of NASDAQHILO		2 weeks	0.58%	0.70%	136	260	52.31%	56.43%
NDX	10-wk low of NASDAQHILO		1 week	1.08%	0.36%	93	154	60.39%	55.51%
NDX	10-wk low of NASDAQHILO		2 weeks	0.70%	0.70%	84	154	54.55%	56.43%
NDX	1-wk high of NASDAQHILO	Above 200-day MA	1 week	0.33%	0.49%	383	677	56.57%	57.45%
NDX	1-wk high of NASDAQHILO	Above 200-day MA	2 weeks	0.84%	1.02%	395	676	58.43%	59.07%
NDX	5-wk high of NASDAQHILO	Above 200-day MA	1 week	0.24%	0.49%	126	236	53.39%	57.45%
NDX	5-wk high of NASDAQHILO	Above 200-day MA	2 weeks	1.08%	1.02%	143	236	60.59%	59.07%
NDX	10-wk high of NASDAQHILO	Above 200-day MA	1 week	0.53%	0.49%	81	154	52.60%	57.45%
NDX	10-wk high of NASDAQHILO	Above 200-day MA	2 weeks	1.75%	1.02%	99	154	64.29%	59.07%
NDX	1-wk low of NASDAQHILO	Above 200-day MA	1 week	0.66%	0.49%	325	547	59.41%	57.45%
NDX	1-wk low of NASDAQHILO	Above 200-day MA	2 weeks	1.25%	1.02%	340	547	62.16%	59.07%
NDX	5-wk low of NASDAQHILO	Above 200-day MA	1 week	0.34%	0.49%	88	163	53.99%	57.45%
NDX	5-wk low of NASDAQHILO	Above 200-day MA	2 weeks	0.99%	1.02%	93	163	57.06%	59.07%
NDX	10-wk low of NASDAQHILO	Above 200-day MA	1 week	0.59%	0.49%	56	97	57.73%	57.45%
NDX	10-wk low of NASDAQHILO	Above 200-day MA	2 weeks	0.89%	1.02%	57	97	58.76%	59.07%
NDX	1-wk high of NASDAQHILO	Below 200-day MA	1 week	0.06%	0.05%	135	260	51.92%	50.99%
NDX	1-wk high of NASDAQHILO	Below 200-day MA	2 weeks	-0.69%	-0.03%	129	260	49.62%	50.28%
NDX	5-wk high of NASDAQHILO	Below 200-day MA	1 week	0.32%	0.05%	32	68	47.06%	50.99%
NDX	5-wk high of NASDAQHILO	Below 200-day MA	2 weeks	-0.18%	-0.03%	35	68	51.47%	50.28%
NDX	10-wk high of NASDAQHILO	Below 200-day MA	1 week	0.47%	0.05%	15	31	48.39%	50.99%
NDX	10-wk high of NASDAQHILO	Below 200-day MA	2 weeks	-0.63%	-0.03%	16	31	51.61%	50.28%
NDX	1-wk low of NASDAQHILO	Below 200-day MA	1 week	0.33%	0.05%	162	295	54.92%	50.99%
NDX	1-wk low of NASDAQHILO	Below 200-day MA	2 weeks	0.21%	-0.03%	147	294	50.00%	50.28%
NDX	5-wk low of NASDAQHILO	Below 200-day MA	1 week	0.85%	0.05%	59	97	60.82%	50.99%
NDX	5-wk low of NASDAQHILO	Below 200-day MA	2 weeks	-0.10%	-0.03%	43	97	44.33%	50.28%
NDX	10-wk low of NASDAQHILO	Below 200-day MA	1 week	0.85%	0.05%	59	97	60.82%	50.99%
NDX	10-wk low of NASDAQHILO	Below 200-day MA	2 weeks	-0.10%	-0.03%	43	97	44.33%	50.28%

SUMMARY AND CONCLUSION

A market making a number of new 52-week highs is usually viewed as bullish, and a market making a number of new 52-week lows is usually viewed as bearish. Over the longer term, this may or may not be true, but when looking at prices over a one-week period, there has been no edge in viewing the market this way.

Now let's move to two popular sentiment indicators: the put/call ratio and the VIX.

CHAPTER **9**

PUT/CALL RATIO

■ ■

We will now look at the put/call ratio, an indicator which is widely used by market professionals.

The put/call ratio is the total number of puts divided by the total number of calls for all index and equity options traded on the Chicago Board of Options Exchange (CBOE). It is widely assumed that the put/call ratio acts as a contrary indicator. High readings (meaning an abundance of put buying versus call buying) supposedly means that there is much fear in the marketplace and that a reversal is likely near. Low readings (lots of call buying or little put buying) means there is complacency and confidence in the marketplace.

Much has been written about this ratio but as far as we know there has been little statistical evidence to specifically confirm what exactly is a "high level" and what is a "low level." Our goal with this research was to confirm the hypothesis and then define the parameters to best exploit the findings.

We looked at three scenarios (all scenarios used closing data). Our first scenario took the data published on the CBOE web site (beginning September 27, 1995 up through year-end 2003). We defined high readings as those that fell in the top 5% and 10% of all the readings and we defined low readings as those that fell in the bottom 5% and 10%. The median reading for the 2077 days we looked at was .68. The top 5% readings were

.97 and higher, the top 10% readings were .90 and higher, the bottom 5% readings were .47 and lower and the bottom 10% readings were .50 and lower.

A summary of our tests is as follows:

High Put/Call Ratios Outperformed Low Put/Call Ratios

1. The top 5% and 10% readings outperformed the benchmark over 1 day, 2 days and 1 week.

2. The bottom 5% and 10% readings underperformed over 2 days and 1 week. In fact, all but one of the time frames lost money in spite of the upward bias of the market. This is further confirmation that complacency exists near short-term tops.

3. High put/call ratios far outperformed low put/call ratios as defined by our parameters. Fear, as defined by a high put/call ratio, has led to greater gains than low put/call readings.

Our second scenario looked at when the 21-day moving average of the ratio made a new 20-day high and a new 20-day low. We used the 21-day average because (for some unknown reason) it has become commonly relied upon in trading circles.

A summary of our findings is as follows:

1. We could not find an edge in this approach. It doesn't mean that some type of edge here doesn't exist when accompanied by other factors. It simply means that as a stand-alone indicator, it has shown no edge over a better-than-8-year period.

The third scenario we looked at was when the put/call ratio made either a 5-day high, a 10-day high, a 5-day low, or a 10-day low. Our findings showed the following:

Short-Term Lows on the Put/Call Ratio Are Followed by Market Underperformance

1. The 5-day lows and the 10-day lows both underperformed the benchmark. In fact, the 10-day lows lost money after a week in both the S&P 500 and the Nasdaq 100. This is good information for profit taking, waiting for long entries, and for potential short selling.

2. There does not seem to be much of an edge when the ratio made a 5-day high or a 10-day high.

3. Both 5- and 10-day highs outperformed 5- and 10-day lows.

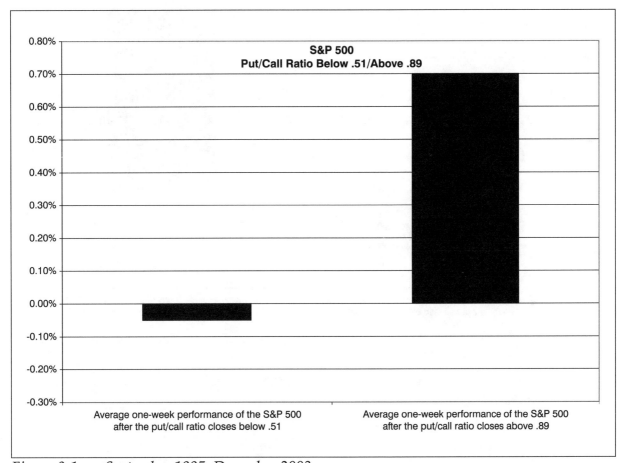

Figure 9-1   *September 1995–December 2003*

High Put/Call Ratios Far Outperformed Low Put/Call Ratios Over 1 Week

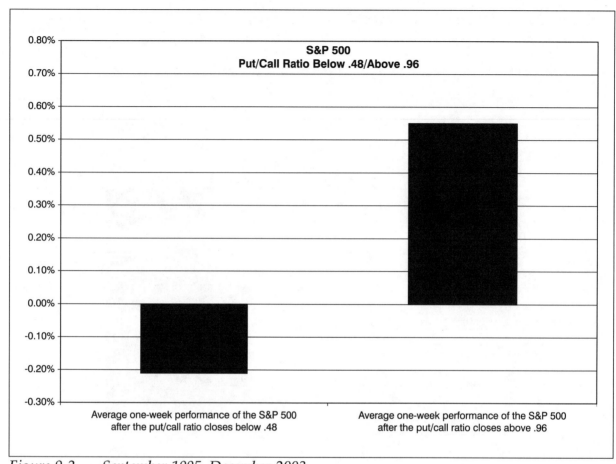

Figure 9-2   *September 1995–December 2003*

Put/Call Ratios Below .48 Have Seen the S&P 500 Decline (on Average) Over the Next Week

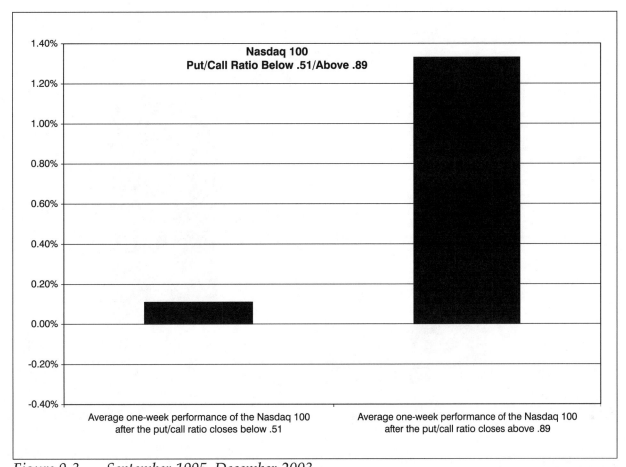

Figure 9-3   September 1995–December 2003

Put/Call Ratios Above .89 Have Seen the Nasdaq Rise Sharply Over the Next Week

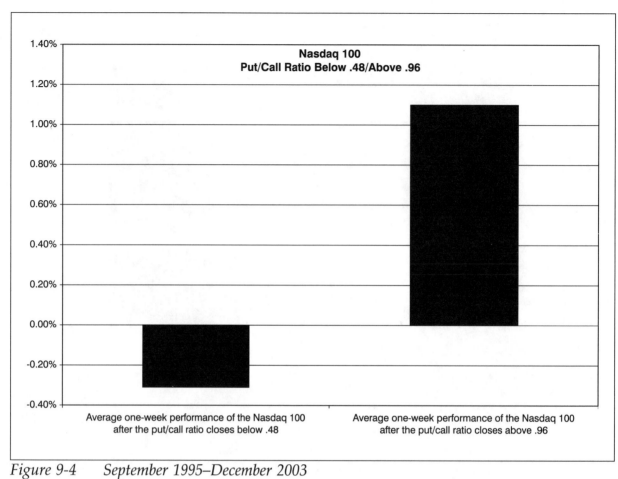

Figure 9-4   *September 1995–December 2003*

Low Put/Call Ratios Have Been Followed by Nasdaq Losses Within 1 Week

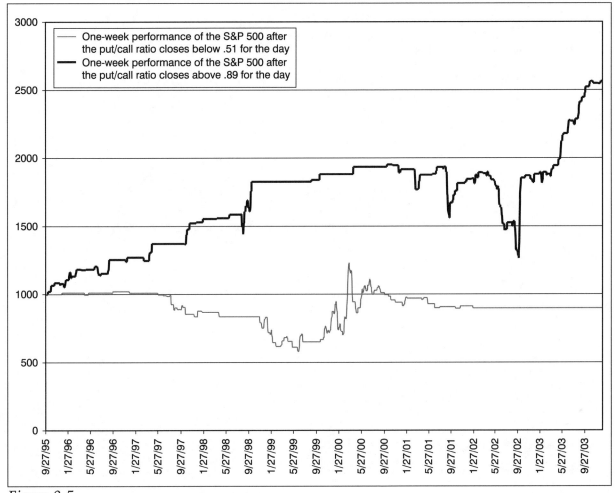

Figure 9-5

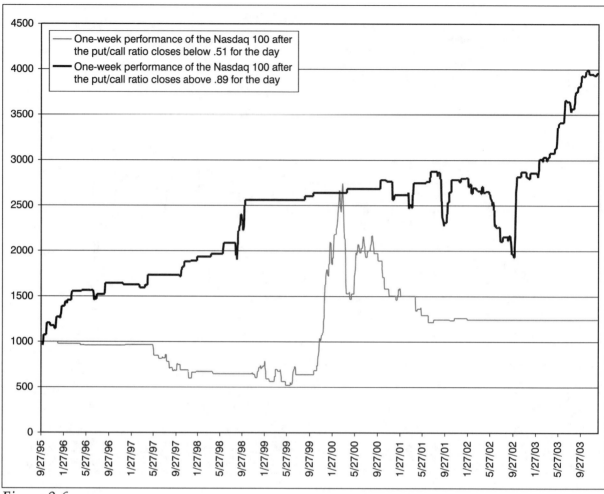

Figure 9-6

Index	Rule	Time Period	Gain/Loss	Benchmark Avg	# Winners	# Days	% Profitable	% Profitable Benchmark
SPX	Today's Put/Call ratio closes > .89	1 day	0.13%	0.04%	122	223	54.71%	51.61%
SPX	Today's Put/Call ratio closes > .89	2 days	0.33%	0.08%	131	223	58.74%	53.93%
SPX	Today's Put/Call ratio closes > .89	1 week	0.70%	0.19%	137	223	61.43%	55.31%
SPX	Today's Put/Call ratio closes > .96	1 day	0.12%	0.04%	59	113	52.21%	51.61%
SPX	Today's Put/Call ratio closes > .96	2 days	0.24%	0.08%	64	113	56.64%	53.93%
SPX	Today's Put/Call ratio closes > .96	1 week	0.55%	0.19%	72	113	63.72%	55.31%
SPX	Today's Put/Call ratio closes < .51	1 day	0.05%	0.04%	111	214	51.87%	51.61%
SPX	Today's Put/Call ratio closes < .51	2 days	-0.05%	0.08%	106	214	49.53%	53.93%
SPX	Today's Put/Call ratio closes < .51	1 week	-0.05%	0.19%	105	214	49.07%	55.31%
SPX	Today's Put/Call ratio closes < .48	1 day	-0.03%	0.04%	56	118	47.46%	51.61%
SPX	Today's Put/Call ratio closes < .48	2 days	-0.09%	0.08%	55	118	46.61%	53.93%
SPX	Today's Put/Call ratio closes < .48	1 week	-0.21%	0.19%	55	118	46.61%	55.31%
SPX	P/C 21-day MA makes a 20-day high	1 day	0.06%	0.04%	200	386	51.81%	51.61%
SPX	P/C 21-day MA makes a 20-day high	2 days	0.13%	0.08%	212	386	54.92%	53.93%
SPX	P/C 21-day MA makes a 20-day high	1 week	0.32%	0.19%	226	386	58.55%	55.31%
SPX	P/C 21-day MA makes a 20-day low	1 day	0.07%	0.04%	221	430	51.40%	51.61%
SPX	P/C 21-day MA makes a 20-day low	2 days	0.06%	0.08%	225	429	52.45%	53.93%
SPX	P/C 21-day MA makes a 20-day low	1 week	0.31%	0.19%	236	428	55.14%	55.31%
SPX	P/C closes at a 5-day high	1 day	-0.02%	0.04%	239	477	50.10%	51.61%
SPX	P/C closes at a 5-day high	2 days	0.05%	0.08%	248	478	51.88%	53.93%
SPX	P/C closes at a 5-day high	1 week	0.21%	0.19%	272	478	56.90%	55.31%
SPX	P/C closes at a 10-day high	1 day	-0.01%	0.04%	127	260	48.85%	51.61%
SPX	P/C closes at a 10-day high	2 days	0.06%	0.08%	134	261	51.34%	53.93%
SPX	P/C closes at a 10-day high	1 week	0.11%	0.19%	144	261	55.17%	55.31%
SPX	P/C closes at a 5-day low	1 day	0.14%	0.04%	266	483	55.07%	51.61%
SPX	P/C closes at a 5-day low	2 days	0.07%	0.08%	266	483	55.07%	53.93%
SPX	P/C closes at a 5-day low	1 week	0.04%	0.19%	260	481	54.05%	55.31%
SPX	P/C closes at a 10-day low	1 day	0.04%	0.04%	138	268	51.49%	51.61%
SPX	P/C closes at a 10-day low	2 days	-0.16%	0.08%	134	268	50.00%	53.93%
SPX	P/C closes at a 10-day low	1 week	-0.32%	0.19%	128	266	48.12%	55.31%

See page 17 for column descriptions.

Index	Rule	Time Period	Gain/Loss	Benchmark Avg	# Winners	# Days	% Profitable	% Profitable Benchmark
NDX	Today's Put/Call ratio closes > .89	1 day	0.35%	0.07%	124	223	55.61%	53.04%
NDX	Today's Put/Call ratio closes > .89	2 days	0.69%	0.15%	130	223	58.30%	52.67%
NDX	Today's Put/Call ratio closes > .89	1 week	1.33%	0.35%	140	223	62.78%	54.44%
NDX	Today's Put/Call ratio closes > .96	1 day	0.26%	0.07%	58	113	51.33%	53.04%
NDX	Today's Put/Call ratio closes > .96	2 days	0.58%	0.15%	64	113	56.64%	52.67%
NDX	Today's Put/Call ratio closes > .96	1 week	1.10%	0.35%	71	113	62.83%	54.44%
NDX	Today's Put/Call ratio closes < .51	1 day	0.15%	0.07%	123	213	57.75%	53.04%
NDX	Today's Put/Call ratio closes < .51	2 days	0.00%	0.15%	115	214	53.74%	52.67%
NDX	Today's Put/Call ratio closes < .51	1 week	0.11%	0.35%	118	214	55.14%	54.44%
NDX	Today's Put/Call ratio closes < .48	1 day	-0.03%	0.07%	64	117	54.70%	53.04%
NDX	Today's Put/Call ratio closes < .48	2 days	-0.16%	0.15%	65	118	55.08%	52.67%
NDX	Today's Put/Call ratio closes < .48	1 week	-0.31%	0.35%	65	118	55.08%	54.44%
NDX	P/C 21-day MA makes a 20-day high	1 day	0.18%	0.07%	203	386	52.59%	53.04%
NDX	P/C 21-day MA makes a 20-day high	2 days	0.32%	0.15%	202	386	52.33%	52.67%
NDX	P/C 21-day MA makes a 20-day high	1 week	0.75%	0.35%	215	386	55.70%	54.44%
NDX	P/C 21-day MA makes a 20-day low	1 day	0.09%	0.07%	234	429	54.55%	53.04%
NDX	P/C 21-day MA makes a 20-day low	2 days	0.08%	0.15%	225	429	52.45%	52.67%
NDX	P/C 21-day MA makes a 20-day low	1 week	0.58%	0.35%	240	428	56.07%	54.44%
NDX	P/C closes at a 5-day high	1 day	0.06%	0.07%	256	478	53.56%	53.04%
NDX	P/C closes at a 5-day high	2 days	0.20%	0.15%	239	478	50.00%	52.67%
NDX	P/C closes at a 5-day high	1 week	0.45%	0.35%	256	478	53.56%	54.44%
NDX	P/C closes at a 10-day high	1 day	0.10%	0.07%	144	261	55.17%	53.04%
NDX	P/C closes at a 10-day high	2 days	0.24%	0.15%	138	261	52.87%	52.67%
NDX	P/C closes at a 10-day high	1 week	0.42%	0.35%	144	261	55.17%	54.44%
NDX	P/C closes at a 5-day low	1 day	0.13%	0.07%	259	482	53.73%	53.04%
NDX	P/C closes at a 5-day low	2 days	-0.02%	0.15%	253	483	52.38%	52.67%
NDX	P/C closes at a 5-day low	1 week	0.10%	0.35%	259	481	53.85%	54.44%
NDX	P/C closes at a 10-day low	1 day	-0.06%	0.07%	123	267	46.07%	53.04%
NDX	P/C closes at a 10-day low	2 days	-0.42%	0.15%	130	268	48.51%	52.67%
NDX	P/C closes at a 10-day low	1 week	-0.49%	0.35%	128	266	48.12%	54.44%

CONCLUSION AND SUMMARY

High put/call ratios have outperformed low put/call ratios, especially if you measure them as we did in the first scenario. Moving average highs and lows by themselves have no edge. As mentioned, there has been an edge over time when one has waited for the put/call ratio to reach extreme historical high levels to be a buyer and extreme historical low levels to be a seller.

Let's now move to another popular indicator which measures market sentiment—the VIX.

CHAPTER **10**

VOLATILITY INDEX (VIX)

■ ■

The CBOE Volatility Index (VIX) is a measurement of the implied volatility of the S&P 500 options. The VIX measures market sentiment and is used by professional traders to gauge the amount of fear and complacency in the marketplace. High VIX readings are usually accompanied by a market that has recently declined and low VIX reading are usually accompanied by a market that has recently risen.

There are a number of ways to use the VIX but before we go into that, we first need to mention how *not* to use it. Over the past decade, many people have used "static" numbers with the VIX. The common theme for many years was to sell the market when the VIX reached the low 20's level and buy the market when it reached 30. Unfortunately, that turned out to be a recipe for disaster (as every other static reading analysis on the VIX has been). In the summer of 2002 the VIX not only crossed 30 and triggered the supposedly magical buy signal, but it proceeded to rise to above 50 over the next few months. The SPX dropped significantly as this buy signal was in place. And then, in late 2003, the VIX went into the low 20's again triggering a magical signal (this time sell), yet the market proceeded to rally and the VIX headed into the teens, leaving these short sellers with substantial losses. *If there is one truism that we've found, it is the fact that static numbers do not work when it comes to the VIX.*

Now, let's look at our tests and see if the VIX can be used to help you time your market entries. We looked at a period from 1990 (the first available calculations from the CBOE for the VIX) through the end of 2003 (14 years). We looked at the VIX as it stretched beyond its 10-day moving average. We used this average to keep the measurement dynamic versus using a static number. This means we are constantly looking at the VIX and comparing it to where it has been on average over the past 10 days versus today.

A summary of the findings is as follows:

When the VIX Has Closed 10% or More Above Its 10-Period Moving Average, the Market Has Made Strong Gains

1. The further the VIX rises above its 10-period moving average, the greater the likelihood that the market will move higher and the greater the likelihood that this market reversal to the upside will be greater than the average daily move of a normal market. We can see this when the VIX closes 5% above its moving average, 10% above its moving average and especially 15% above its moving average. The edge is fairly consistent over a 1-day period, a 2-day period and a 1-week period. In fact the 1-week gain in the SPX when the VIX is 10% above its 10-day moving average is more than *double* the average weekly gain over the 14-year period.

The VIX Closing 5% or More Below Its 10-Period Moving Average Has Seen the Market Make Little Progress Over the Next Week

2. When the VIX closes more than 5% below its 10-period moving average, the market has greatly underperformed the averages. In fact, in some cases the market lost money over the short term. This finding is extremely significant because it identifies the times when the least amount of money has been made over the past 14 years. For example, over the 14-year period, the VIX has closed 5% under its 10-period moving average approximately 25% of the time (1123 days). The SPX rose over 300% over this 14-year period but none of the cumulative net weekly gains have occurred while the VIX closed 5% under its 10-period moving average. This information confirms that the VIX can identify overbought markets and helps you identify the times that you should be aggressive in locking in gains and/or avoiding long purchases.

The Nasdaq Behavior Has Approximately Mirrored the S&P 500 Behavior When the VIX Has Been Stretched

3. We did not look at the VXN, which is the Nasdaq version of the VIX because the data only went back to 2001. But, we did look at how the Nasdaq performed when the VIX closed above and below its 10-period moving average. It was interesting to see how the results carried over into the Nasdaq. The Nasdaq's average daily, 2-day, and 1-week gain significantly improved when the VIX was 5% and 10% above its moving average. And the Nasdaq underperformed when the VIX closed 5% and 10% below its moving average. These findings further confirm the significance of the VIX in guiding you when to enter the market, when not to enter the market and when to be more aggressive in locking in both long and short gains.

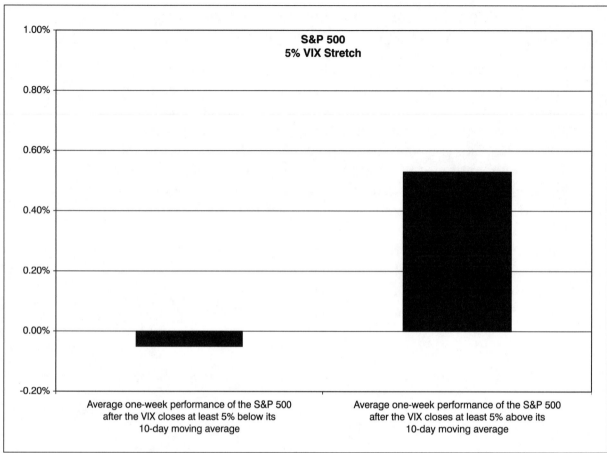

Figure 10-1   1990–2003

The Market on Average Has Made Little Progress Within a Week When the VIX Has Closed at Least 5% Below Its 10-Period Moving Average

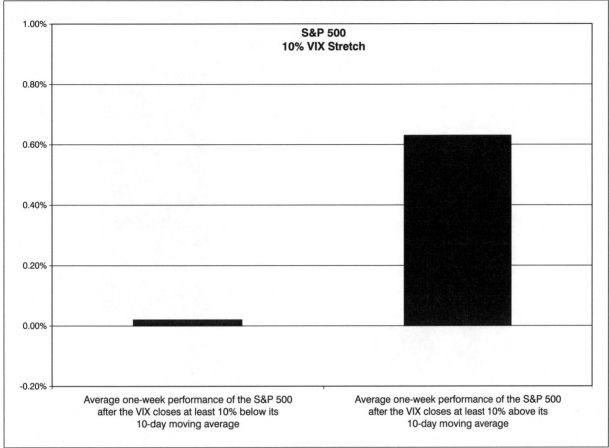

Figure 10-2   *1990–2003*

The Market Has Outperformed During the Times the VIX Has Closed 10% or More Above Its 10-Period Moving Average. The Opposite Is True When It Has Closed 10% or More Below Its 10-Period Moving Average.

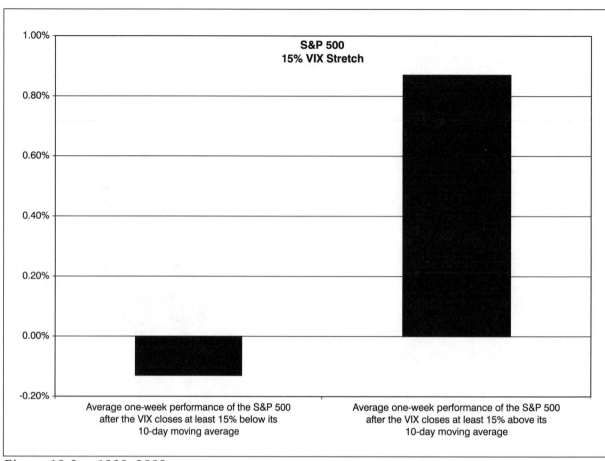

Figure 10-3   1990–2003

15% VIX Stretches to the Upside (Though Rare) Have Been Followed by Strong Market Gains

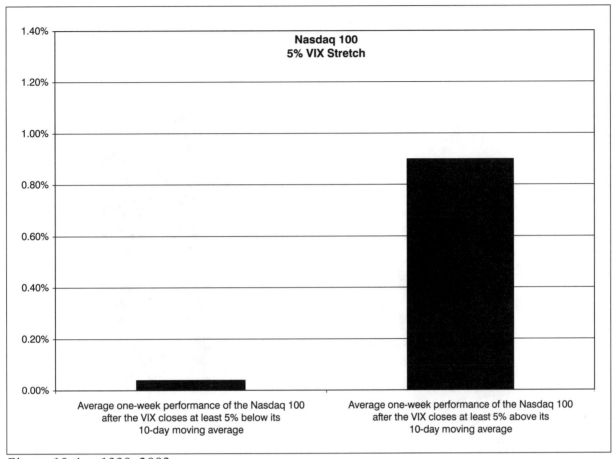

Figure 10-4   *1990–2003*
            The Nasdaq Has Shown Much Stronger Gains Over 1 Week When the VIX Has Closed 5% Above Its 10-Period Moving Average versus 5% Below

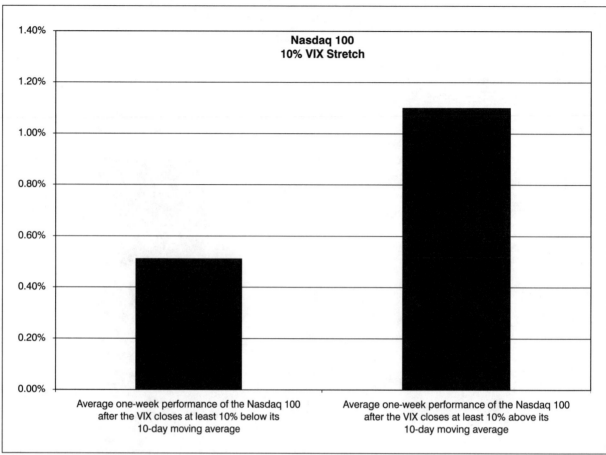

Figure 10-5   1990–2003

10% VIX Stretches Above Its 10-Period Moving Average Have Outperformed 10% VIX Stretches Below Its 10-Period Moving Average by Approximately a 2:1 Margin

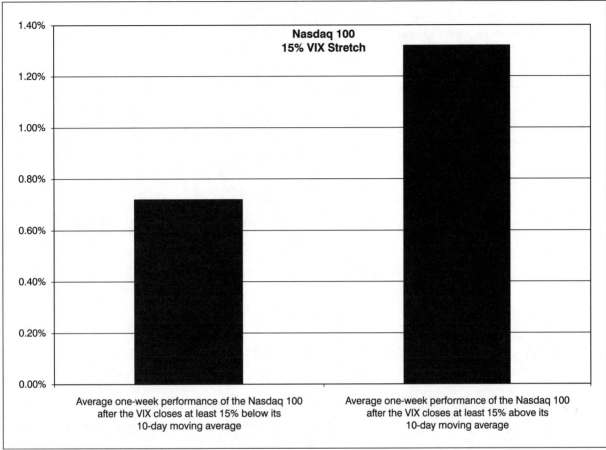

Figure 10-6   1990–2003

When the VIX Has Closed 15% Above Its 10-Period Moving Average, the Nasdaq Has Proceeded to Rally Strongly Over the Next Week

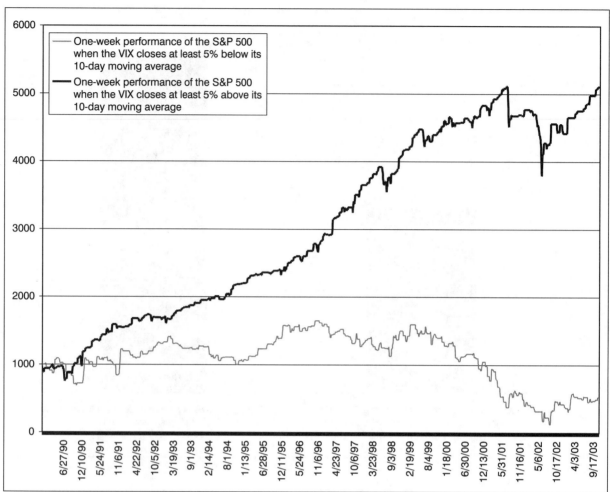

Figure 10-7

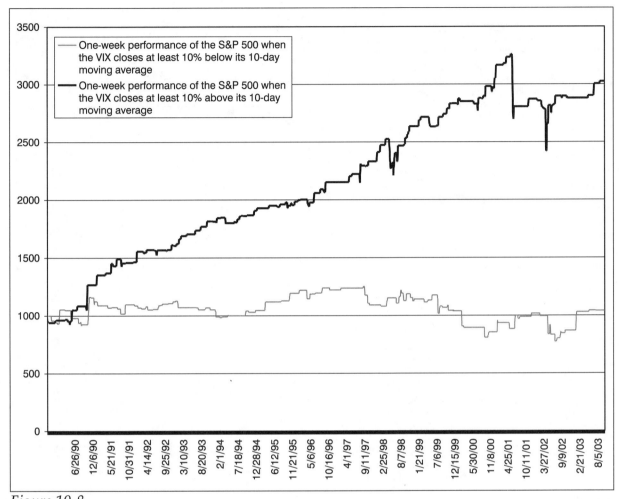

Figure 10-8

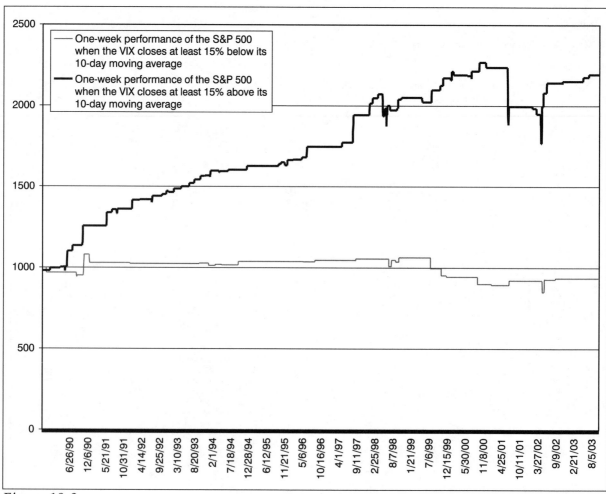

Figure 10-9

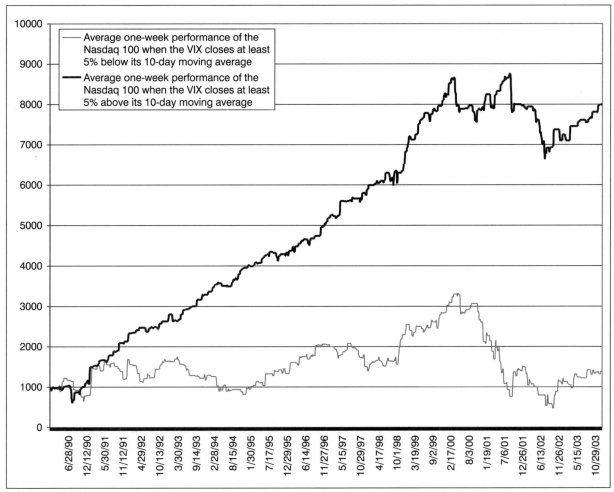

Figure 10-10

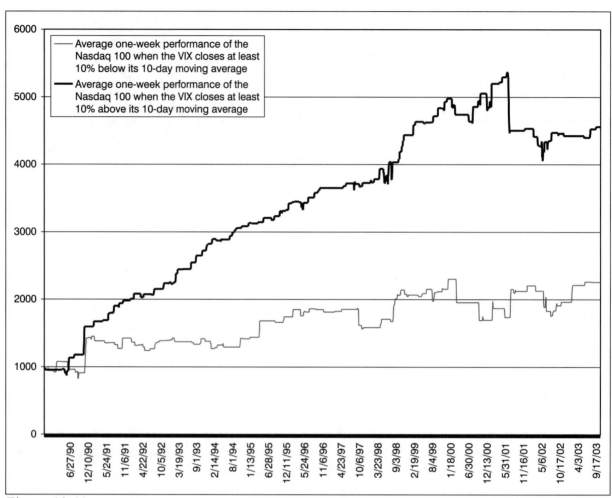

Figure 10-11

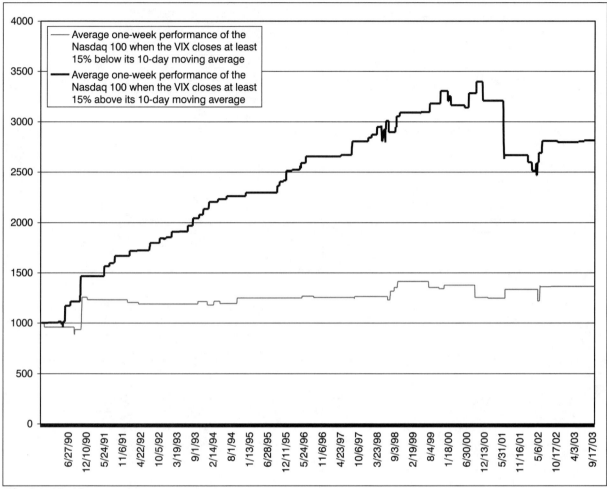

Figure 10-12

Index	Rule 1	Rule 2	Time Period	Gain/Loss	Benchmark Avg	# Winners	# Days	% Profitable	% Profitable Benchmark
SPX	Within 2%		1 day	0.02%	0.04%	409	758	53.96%	52.27%
SPX	Within 2%		2 days	0.04%	0.08%	398	758	52.51%	53.89%
SPX	Within 2%		1 week	0.12%	0.19%	416	757	54.95%	56.05%
SPX	5% above		1 day	0.08%	0.04%	423	779	54.30%	52.27%
SPX	5% above		2 days	0.19%	0.08%	432	779	55.46%	53.89%
SPX	5% above		1 week	0.53%	0.19%	469	778	60.28%	56.05%
SPX	10% above		1 day	0.09%	0.04%	178	323	55.11%	52.27%
SPX	10% above		2 days	0.23%	0.08%	190	323	58.82%	53.89%
SPX	10% above		1 week	0.63%	0.19%	202	323	62.54%	56.05%
SPX	15% above		1 day	0.37%	0.04%	86	137	62.77%	52.27%
SPX	15% above		2 days	0.61%	0.08%	94	137	68.61%	53.89%
SPX	15% above		1 week	0.87%	0.19%	92	137	67.15%	56.05%
SPX	5% below		1 day	0.01%	0.04%	425	875	48.57%	52.27%
SPX	5% below		2 days	-0.01%	0.08%	455	875	52.00%	53.89%
SPX	5% below		1 week	-0.05%	0.19%	461	876	52.63%	56.05%
SPX	10% below		1 day	0.11%	0.04%	133	246	54.07%	52.27%
SPX	10% below		2 days	0.03%	0.08%	131	247	53.04%	53.89%
SPX	10% below		1 week	0.02%	0.19%	133	247	53.85%	56.05%
SPX	15% below		1 day	0.06%	0.04%	27	51	52.94%	52.27%
SPX	15% below		2 days	-0.02%	0.08%	24	51	47.06%	53.89%
SPX	15% below		1 week	-0.13%	0.19%	28	51	54.90%	56.05%
SPX	Within 2%	Above the 200-day MA	1 day	0.03%	0.05%	309	564	54.79%	52.95%
SPX	Within 2%	Above the 200-day MA	2 days	0.07%	0.10%	300	564	53.19%	55.40%
SPX	Within 2%	Above the 200-day MA	1 week	0.20%	0.24%	314	563	55.77%	57.53%
SPX	5% above	Above the 200-day MA	1 day	0.11%	0.05%	283	498	56.83%	52.95%
SPX	5% above	Above the 200-day MA	2 days	0.22%	0.10%	287	498	57.63%	55.40%
SPX	5% above	Above the 200-day MA	1 week	0.57%	0.24%	314	497	63.18%	57.53%
SPX	10% above	Above the 200-day MA	1 day	0.12%	0.05%	106	177	59.89%	52.95%
SPX	10% above	Above the 200-day MA	2 days	0.31%	0.10%	113	177	63.84%	55.40%
SPX	10% above	Above the 200-day MA	1 week	0.69%	0.24%	117	177	66.10%	57.53%
SPX	15% above	Above the 200-day MA	1 day	0.46%	0.05%	46	71	64.79%	52.95%
SPX	15% above	Above the 200-day MA	2 days	0.65%	0.10%	50	71	70.42%	55.40%
SPX	15% above	Above the 200-day MA	1 week	0.99%	0.24%	54	71	76.06%	57.53%
SPX	5% below	Above the 200-day MA	1 day	0.01%	0.05%	298	617	48.30%	52.95%
SPX	5% below	Above the 200-day MA	2 days	0.02%	0.10%	331	617	53.65%	55.40%
SPX	5% below	Above the 200-day MA	1 week	-0.01%	0.24%	328	618	53.07%	57.53%
SPX	10% below	Above the 200-day MA	1 day	0.06%	0.05%	79	154	51.30%	52.95%
SPX	10% below	Above the 200-day MA	2 days	-0.05%	0.10%	79	155	50.97%	55.40%
SPX	10% below	Above the 200-day MA	1 week	-0.14%	0.24%	77	155	49.68%	57.53%
SPX	15% below	Above the 200-day MA	1 day	-0.10%	0.05%	9	23	39.13%	52.95%
SPX	15% below	Above the 200-day MA	2 days	-0.33%	0.10%	8	23	34.78%	55.40%
SPX	15% below	Above the 200-day MA	1 week	-0.66%	0.24%	11	23	47.83%	57.53%
SPX	Within 2%	Below the 200-day MA	1 day	-0.03%	0.02%	100	194	51.55%	50.63%
SPX	Within 2%	Below the 200-day MA	2 days	-0.05%	0.04%	98	194	50.52%	50.24%
SPX	Within 2%	Below the 200-day MA	1 week	-0.11%	0.09%	102	194	52.58%	52.48%
SPX	5% above	Below the 200-day MA	1 day	0.02%	0.02%	140	281	49.82%	50.63%
SPX	5% above	Below the 200-day MA	2 days	0.14%	0.04%	145	281	51.60%	50.24%
SPX	5% above	Below the 200-day MA	1 week	0.45%	0.09%	155	281	55.16%	52.48%
SPX	10% above	Below the 200-day MA	1 day	0.07%	0.02%	72	146	49.32%	50.63%
SPX	10% above	Below the 200-day MA	2 days	0.14%	0.04%	77	146	52.74%	50.24%
SPX	10% above	Below the 200-day MA	1 week	0.55%	0.09%	85	146	58.22%	52.48%
SPX	15% above	Below the 200-day MA	1 day	0.27%	0.02%	40	66	60.61%	50.63%
SPX	15% above	Below the 200-day MA	2 days	0.57%	0.04%	44	66	66.67%	50.24%
SPX	15% above	Below the 200-day MA	1 week	0.75%	0.09%	38	66	57.58%	52.48%
SPX	5% below	Below the 200-day MA	1 day	0.01%	0.02%	127	258	49.22%	50.63%
SPX	5% below	Below the 200-day MA	2 days	-0.07%	0.04%	124	258	48.06%	50.24%
SPX	5% below	Below the 200-day MA	1 week	-0.16%	0.09%	133	258	51.55%	52.48%
SPX	10% below	Below the 200-day MA	1 day	0.18%	0.02%	54	92	58.70%	50.63%
SPX	10% below	Below the 200-day MA	2 days	0.15%	0.04%	52	92	56.52%	50.24%
SPX	10% below	Below the 200-day MA	1 week	0.29%	0.09%	56	92	60.87%	52.48%
SPX	15% below	Below the 200-day MA	1 day	0.19%	0.02%	18	28	64.29%	50.63%
SPX	15% below	Below the 200-day MA	2 days	0.24%	0.04%	16	28	57.14%	50.24%
SPX	15% below	Below the 200-day MA	1 week	0.31%	0.09%	17	28	60.71%	52.48%

See page 17 for column descriptions.

Index	Rule 1	Rule 2	Time Period	Gain/Loss	Benchmark Avg	# Winners	# Days	% Profitable	% Profitable Benchmark
NDX	Within 2%		1 day	0.03%	0.08%	419	758	55.28%	53.85%
NDX	Within 2%		2 days	0.10%	0.15%	398	758	52.51%	53.10%
NDX	Within 2%		1 week	0.32%	0.37%	422	757	55.75%	55.63%
NDX	5% above		1 day	0.22%	0.08%	427	777	54.95%	53.85%
NDX	5% above		2 days	0.42%	0.15%	434	779	55.71%	53.10%
NDX	5% above		1 week	0.90%	0.37%	480	778	61.70%	55.63%
NDX	10% above		1 day	0.39%	0.08%	187	322	58.07%	53.85%
NDX	10% above		2 days	0.71%	0.15%	193	323	59.75%	53.10%
NDX	10% above		1 week	1.10%	0.37%	211	323	65.33%	55.63%
NDX	15% above		1 day	0.89%	0.08%	94	136	69.12%	53.85%
NDX	15% above		2 days	1.32%	0.15%	96	137	70.07%	53.10%
NDX	15% above		1 week	1.32%	0.37%	102	137	74.45%	55.63%
NDX	5% below		1 day	0.03%	0.08%	460	874	52.63%	53.85%
NDX	5% below		2 days	0.04%	0.15%	463	875	52.91%	53.10%
NDX	5% below		1 week	0.04%	0.37%	461	876	52.63%	55.63%
NDX	10% below		1 day	0.27%	0.08%	141	247	57.09%	53.85%
NDX	10% below		2 days	0.18%	0.15%	129	246	52.44%	53.10%
NDX	10% below		1 week	0.51%	0.37%	143	247	57.89%	55.63%
NDX	15% below		1 day	0.22%	0.08%	26	51	50.98%	53.85%
NDX	15% below		2 days	0.21%	0.15%	27	51	52.94%	53.10%
NDX	15% below		1 week	0.72%	0.37%	30	51	58.82%	55.63%
NDX	Within 2%	Above the 200-day MA	1 day	0.07%	0.09%	318	560	56.79%	54.65%
NDX	Within 2%	Above the 200-day MA	2 days	0.16%	0.20%	299	560	53.39%	54.52%
NDX	Within 2%	Above the 200-day MA	1 week	0.47%	0.50%	323	559	57.78%	57.61%
NDX	5% above	Above the 200-day MA	1 day	0.18%	0.09%	272	490	55.51%	54.65%
NDX	5% above	Above the 200-day MA	2 days	0.40%	0.20%	278	490	56.73%	54.52%
NDX	5% above	Above the 200-day MA	1 week	0.99%	0.50%	321	489	65.64%	57.61%
NDX	10% above	Above the 200-day MA	1 day	0.23%	0.09%	108	184	58.70%	54.65%
NDX	10% above	Above the 200-day MA	2 days	0.60%	0.20%	112	184	60.87%	54.52%
NDX	10% above	Above the 200-day MA	1 week	1.20%	0.50%	128	184	69.57%	57.61%
NDX	15% above	Above the 200-day MA	1 day	0.86%	0.09%	53	78	67.95%	54.65%
NDX	15% above	Above the 200-day MA	2 days	1.09%	0.20%	53	78	67.95%	54.52%
NDX	15% above	Above the 200-day MA	1 week	1.56%	0.50%	61	78	78.21%	57.61%
NDX	5% below	Above the 200-day MA	1 day	0.08%	0.09%	327	614	53.26%	54.65%
NDX	5% below	Above the 200-day MA	2 days	0.15%	0.20%	335	614	54.56%	54.52%
NDX	5% below	Above the 200-day MA	1 week	0.33%	0.50%	330	615	53.66%	57.61%
NDX	10% below	Above the 200-day MA	1 day	0.29%	0.09%	94	161	58.39%	54.65%
NDX	10% below	Above the 200-day MA	2 days	0.24%	0.20%	87	160	54.38%	54.52%
NDX	10% below	Above the 200-day MA	1 week	0.77%	0.50%	99	161	61.49%	57.61%
NDX	15% below	Above the 200-day MA	1 day	0.05%	0.09%	14	30	46.67%	54.65%
NDX	15% below	Above the 200-day MA	2 days	0.27%	0.20%	17	30	56.67%	54.52%
NDX	15% below	Above the 200-day MA	1 week	1.46%	0.50%	20	30	66.67%	57.61%
NDX	Within 2%	Below the 200-day MA	1 day	-0.10%	0.03%	101	198	51.01%	52.00%
NDX	Within 2%	Below the 200-day MA	2 days	-0.06%	0.04%	99	198	50.00%	49.76%
NDX	Within 2%	Below the 200-day MA	1 week	-0.09%	0.05%	99	198	50.00%	51.00%
NDX	5% above	Below the 200-day MA	1 day	0.29%	0.03%	155	287	54.01%	52.00%
NDX	5% above	Below the 200-day MA	2 days	0.45%	0.04%	156	289	53.98%	49.76%
NDX	5% above	Below the 200-day MA	1 week	0.75%	0.05%	159	289	55.02%	51.00%
NDX	10% above	Below the 200-day MA	1 day	0.60%	0.03%	79	138	57.25%	52.00%
NDX	10% above	Below the 200-day MA	2 days	0.85%	0.04%	81	139	58.27%	49.76%
NDX	10% above	Below the 200-day MA	1 week	0.97%	0.05%	83	139	59.71%	51.00%
NDX	15% above	Below the 200-day MA	1 day	0.93%	0.03%	41	58	70.69%	52.00%
NDX	15% above	Below the 200-day MA	2 days	1.63%	0.04%	43	59	72.88%	49.76%
NDX	15% above	Below the 200-day MA	1 week	1.02%	0.05%	41	59	69.49%	51.00%
NDX	5% below	Below the 200-day MA	1 day	-0.08%	0.03%	133	260	51.15%	52.00%
NDX	5% below	Below the 200-day MA	2 days	-0.24%	0.04%	128	261	49.04%	49.76%
NDX	5% below	Below the 200-day MA	1 week	-0.64%	0.05%	131	261	50.19%	51.00%
NDX	10% below	Below the 200-day MA	1 day	0.23%	0.03%	47	86	54.65%	52.00%
NDX	10% below	Below the 200-day MA	2 days	0.06%	0.04%	42	86	48.84%	49.76%
NDX	10% below	Below the 200-day MA	1 week	0.02%	0.05%	44	86	51.16%	51.00%
NDX	15% below	Below the 200-day MA	1 day	0.45%	0.03%	12	21	57.14%	52.00%
NDX	15% below	Below the 200-day MA	2 days	0.11%	0.04%	10	21	47.62%	49.76%
NDX	15% below	Below the 200-day MA	1 week	-0.35%	0.05%	10	21	47.62%	51.00%

SUMMARY AND CONCLUSION

In summary, the VIX acts as a barometer to guide you as to how aggressive you should be on the long side, short side, locking in long gains and locking in short gains. As the VIX moves further above its moving average, the likelihood of a market rally increases. The opposite is true when it moves further below its 10-period moving average. As you can see from the time charts, these finding have been fairly consistent and steady for the past 14 years.

CHAPTER 11

USING THE INFORMATION IN THIS BOOK

■ ■

By now we suspect you realize that a lot of the information found in this book flies in the face conventional wisdom. In Chapter 1 we discussed how Bill James' findings, chronicled by Michael Lewis in *Moneyball,* and now successfully used by a number of baseball teams, defied decades of thinking in the baseball world. The findings in this book do the same for the financial world. Just as old school baseball attempted to use the imprecise art of gut and intuition to make decisions, Wall Street and the media does the same when it comes to interpreting markets. Decades of lore, repeated over and over again has become fact, without a shred of quantitative evidence. And, as we have seen from the behavior of the market over the past one and one half decades, much of what is thought to be true is simply wrong. The statistics prove this out.

There is a wealth of information in this book. And there are many ways you can use this information. But, one theme that is very, very obvious is that there has been one consistent way that the market has worked over the past 15 years. *It is that buying market weakness has been superior to buying strength. And it also is very apparent that selling into strength has been better than selling into weakness.* We came to these conclusions after we looked at the market using some of the most popular indicators.

These conclusions were confirmed many different ways, by comparing multiple-days' highs to multiple-days' lows; comparing multiple days of the market rising to multiple days of the market declining; comparing multiple days of the markets rising higher intraday to declining lower intraday; looking at the days when the market rose strongly to the days it declined sharply; studying days when advancing issues were much stronger than declining issues; looking at the put/call ratio, and studying the effects of prices when VIX stretched to extremes. The test results, many using over 3,500 days of trading, all point us in the same direction—it has been smarter, wiser, and more profitable to be buying weakness and selling strength in stocks, than vice versa.

There are no assurances that any of these findings will hold up in the future. There is no guarantee of the market ever acting in any one manner. But, if the past history does hold, there are edges here for you to consider in your trading and short-term investing.

How can you use these results? One could probably write multiple books on this, but we'll provide you with some direction.

1. Should you decide to apply this research to your trading, **you should not use any of these indicators blindly and without stops.** No matter how big the edge has been during some of these times, there have also been large drawdowns in many along the way. Prudent money management and portfolio management (risk control and position size) is a must. In fact, they may be as important if not more important as any trading strategy.

2. We used static time frames for the exit (this means in most cases we used one day, two day and one week exits). The results can likely be improved by using dynamic exits such as price movement or with additional indicators. Again, this is something we encourage you to pursue further. An example is buying the SPX when it hits a new 10-day low and is above its 200-day moving average. By exiting on the close of the day the SPX closed above its 10-day simple moving average, you would have made 797.31 points (hypothetical with no slippage and commission). 80.87% of the trades were profitable with the average gain of .87% per trade. You are only in the market 19% of the time. One can potentially find hundreds of combinations such as this one within this book.

3. If you believe that markets move from overbought to oversold and oversold to overbought, you will want to structure your entire thought process around this. This means looking to be buying the times when the market has had a statistical edge to the long side and looking to exit when the edge is exhausted. This is especially true in bull markets, meaning markets that are trading above their 200-day moving average. And, if you short stocks, you should be looking to be a seller when the market has shown strength, especially when it's trading below its 200-day moving average. As you have seen, historically this has been where some of the biggest edges have existed.

4. Having multiple signals indicating the same thing will likely improve the performance of many of the indicators. We gave you the results of these indicators as they stood alone. We encourage you to use them in combination.

5. Based on the results in this book (along with our own observations) we personally will likely never buy short-term strength again, nor sell short into short-term weakness. And, if we have our way, our kids and their kids never will either. To us, the statistics are too strong to do otherwise.

6. What about fundamental analysis? Good question. We were only looking at the validity of common entry techniques and indicators. Fundamentals may improve results but what has always been interesting to us is the fact that fundamentals are probably one of the easiest areas to test, as the information is vast. Yet in spite of the fact that Wall Street research (both from the brokerage firms and the independent research firms) is overwhelmingly fundamentally driven, there still remains today *little quantified evidence* that their research actually has a statistical edge.

7. Our research focused only on looking at the market over the very short-term. Successful short-term trading is made up of taking advantage of small edges and executing properly from there. It's very difficult to make money trading if you're buying into periods that have historically produced negative returns.

8. We've touched upon this fact throughout the book and we need to touch on it again. Don't get caught up in the hype, especially the hype that the media creates, when the market is very strong or when it's very weak. The press has a habit after a few down days of quoting analysts who pronounce that "the market is breaking down," "things

look bad," "the breadth is terrible," etc. And after the market has had a number of strong up-days, just the opposite happens: They're jumping up and down with excitement. *Markets absolutely do not move in one direction neither short-term nor long term.* They move from overbought to oversold and vice versa (this has been shown over and over again throughout this book). Yes, there has been a 100-year upward long-term bias but it's filled with times the market has sold off and sometimes sold off sharply. You only have to think back a few years to 2000–2002 to know this. If strength was always followed by strength the market would be at infinity, not at the 10,500 level as of this writing. And if weakness always followed through, we would be at zero. Sorry, not only is the concept that strong markets always lead to strong markets illogical, but this book statistically proves otherwise. The media and the analysts most times have it wrong, especially at extremes.

Once again, the stock market moves from overbought to oversold and vice versa, over and over again. The statistics prove this out. It's happened in one way or another for the past 100 years and in our opinion, it will happen for the next 100 years. The key from here is to "properly identify" when the market really is overbought and when it really is oversold. Hopefully, this book solidifies the process of getting you there.

SPECIAL REPORTS

The following reports will provide you with specific strategies to trade the concepts from this book. Many of these strategies have up to 15 years of historical back-tested results, which quantify their potential effectiveness. Each report is written in a simple to understand style and nearly all of the information can be applied immediately to your trading.

Applying How Markets Really Work to Trade the SPYs, QQQ, and SMHs $200

Applying How Markets Really Work to the Options Market— An In-depth Strategy Guide $200

How Markets Really Work—Strategies to Trade the E-mini Market $200

All 3 Reports-$500

To order call toll free 1-888-484-8220 Ext 1. or go to

www.TradersGalleria.com

ABOUT THE AUTHORS

Laurence A. Connors is the managing director and founder of Connors Capital LLC, based in Los Angeles, California. He is also Chairman, CEO and co-founder of The Connors Group, Inc. The Connors Group, Inc. is a financial markets publishing company which publishes daily commentary and insight concerning the financial markets.

Mr. Connors has authored top-selling books on market strategies and volatility trading, including *Street Smarts* (co-authored with Linda Raschke), *Investment Secrets of a Hedge Fund Manager, Connors On Advanced Trading Strategies* and *Trading Connors VIX Reversals.* *Street Smarts* was selected by *Technical Analysis of Stocks and Commodities* magazine as one of "The Classics" for trading books written in the past century. His books have been published in German, Italian, Russian and Japanese.

Mr. Connors' opinions and insights have been featured or quoted in: *The Wall Street Journal; The New York Times; Barron's; Bloomberg Television; Bloomberg Radio; Dow Jones Newswire; Yahoo Finance Vision; Los Angeles Times; E-Trade Financial Daily; Futures Magazine; Technical Analysis of Stocks and Commodities;* and others.

Conor Sen is a Reasearch Analyst with Connors Capital LLC. He has dual degrees in computer science and economics from Harvey Mudd College.